AnimalWays

Spiders

AnimalWays

Spiders

MARC ZABLUDOFF

Marshall Cavendish
Benchmark
New York

With thanks to Dr. Dan Wharton, director of the Central Park Wildlife
Center, for his expert reading of this manuscript.

Marshall Cavendish Benchmark
99 White Plains Road
Tarrytown, NY 10591-9001
Website: www.marshallcavendish.us

All Internet sites were available and accurate when sent to press.

Library of Congress Cataloging-in-Publication Data

Zabludoff, Marc.
Spiders / by Marc Zabludoff.
p. cm. — (Animalways)
Includes bibliographical references and index.
ISBN 0-7614-1747-8
1. Spiders—Juvenile literature. I. Title. II. Series.

QL458.4.Z33 2004
595.4'4—dc22
2004016681

Photo Research by Candlepants Incorporated

Cover Photo: ThinkStock/SuperStock

The photographs in this book are used by permission and through the courtesy of: *Corbis*:
Kevin R. Morris, 2; Kevin Schafer, 9, 75; George H. H. Huey, 14; Michael and Patricia
Fogden, 15, 24, 54, 93; John M. Roberts, 16; Historical Picture Archive, 17; James Leynse,
18; Jonathon Blair, 21; William Dow, 25; Papilio/Steve Austin, 27; Papilio/Clive Druett, 38,
46; Jim Zuckerman, 45 (top), 47; Joe McDonald, 45 (bottom), 69, 90; Gallo Images/Anthony
Bannister, 52, 85, 92, 95; Gallo Images/Carl Hughes, 57; Hal Horwitz, 60; Gary W. Carter, 63;
Chris Hellier, 83; Papilio/Jamie Harron, 88; George McCarthy, back cover; *Scala/Art
Resource, NY*: 12; *Peter Arnold, Inc*: Ed Reschke, 31; Hans Pfletschinger, 36, 80; C. Allen
Morgan, 51; John Cancalosi, 79; Gunter Ziesler, 101; *Minden Pictures*: Mark Moffett, 49;
Michael and Paticia Fogden, 77; *Mark Cassino/SuperStock*: 65; *Getty/AFP*: 97, 99.

Printed in China

1 3 5 6 4 2

Contents

Animal Kingdom

CNIDARIANS

coral

ARTHROPODS
(animals with jointed limbs and external skeleton)

MOLLUSKS

squid

CRUSTACEANS

crab

ARACHNIDS

SPIDER

INSECTS

grasshopper

MYRIAPODS

centipede

CARNIVORES

lion

SEA MAMMALS

whale

PRIMATES

orangutan

HERBIVORES
(5 orders)

elephant

PHYLA

ANNELIDS

earthworm

CHORDATES
(animals with
a dorsal
nerve chord)

ECHINODERMS

starfish

SUB PHYLA

VERTEBRATES
(animals with a
backbone)

CLASSES

FISH

fish

BIRDS

gull

MAMMALS

AMPHIBIANS

frog

REPTILES

snake

ORDERS

RODENTS

squirrel

INSECTIVORES

mole

MARSUPIALS

koala

SMALL MAMMALS
(several orders)

bat

Ancient
Hunters

A delicately painted orange spider hangs head down in the center of a circular web. The web is poised in a broad-leafed tree overlooking a flower-filled garden. It is the middle of a morning in late summer, and the web, finished just an hour ago, nearly shimmers in the sunlight. The sky is a breathtaking blue, the leaves a deep rich green. The spider notices none of this. Its sight is poor; the images it sees, fuzzy.

Thin hairs on the spider's long black-banded legs begin to tremble ever so slightly. Immediately, the spider is alert. The hairs are sensing the movement of air as a nearby insect's tissue-thin wings beat up and down. The wings are coming closer. Suddenly, the web lines stretch and twist. Every millimeter of the spider's body bristles. A tremor races along the spokes of the web, through the spider's clawed feet, along its legs, and straight to its tiny brain. The vibrations are irregular, frantic. They are coming

A GREEN SPIDER DEVOURS A MONARCH BUTTERFLY WITH RELENTLESS EFFICIENCY. THE SPIDER'S HUNTING METHODS INSPIRE FEAR AND REVULSION IN MANY PEOPLE.

from the upper right of the web, two-thirds of the way out toward the edge. Even before the web starts to rock violently, the spider has pivoted. In a blur, its hooked claws glide over the silk threads, following the tremor backward to its source—a fly desperately trying to tug itself free of the glue droplets that hold it tight. The spider reaches out, touches the fly gently, identifying it, tasting it. The spider opens its jaws. Fangs slide out and nip the insect at the joint below its head. Poison flows into the fly's body. In seconds the rocking of the web has ceased. The spider wraps the fly lovingly in silk and pours digestive juices into the silk-wrapped package. As the fly turns to liquid, the beautiful spider begins to dine.

Age-old Inhabitants

Spiders are ancient animals. Their direct ancestors were among the very first animals to crawl out of the sea 400 million years ago and try out life on land. Over that vast stretch of centuries, spiders have taken on many different forms and taken up residence in a vast multitude of places.

There are some 38,000 species, or distinct kinds, of spiders alive today that scientists have named and studied. But the true number is certainly much larger. Perhaps two or three times more species of spiders actually exist. Most dwell in the hidden reaches of tropical rain forests, unseen and unknown by humans. As the forests are cut down to make room for houses, farms, and ranches, many of these spiders will probably become extinct without our ever learning of them.

No one knows how many individual spiders exist on Earth at any given moment. It is difficult to figure out even how many spiders live in a particular acre of the planet. Estimates have ranged from 11,000 per acre in a wood near Washington, D.C., to more than 250,000 per acre in a Panamanian forest to a whopping 2.5 million per acre in an English meadow. That last figure leads to an estimate of more than 2 *trillion*—2,000,000,000,000—spiders in England alone. Worldwide, the figure is simply staggering.

Most of the spiders in an English meadow are tiny. They measure just a tenth of an inch (2.5 mm) from end to end. The smallest known spider is only a fifth that size, just two hundredths of an inch (.5 mm). The biggest, the Goliath birdeater tarantula, has a body length approaching 4 inches (10 cm) and a Frisbee-size leg span of 11 inches (28 cm).

Obviously, spiders are a varied bunch, and they lead diverse lives. Over the eons they have learned to exploit every habitat available. They live in steamy forests and scorching deserts; in grassy plains and fetid swamps; on rocky, wave-battered beaches and mossy riverbanks; in Earth's darkest, deepest caves and atop its highest ice-clad mountains—as high as 22,000 feet above sea level, on Mount Everest. They live wherever they can find food. Since they mostly eat insects, they live virtually everywhere.

Woven Tales

People around the world seem to hold two opposite views of spiders, and their folktales, myths, and superstitions reflect this. On the one hand, we admire spiders for their superb skill in weaving complicated webs of silk. On the other hand, we see spiders as devious and dangerous. The mere sight of even a penny-size eight-legged beast is enough to send many a person screaming in panic-stricken flight.

In European culture, spider tales date back to the myths of the ancient Greeks, and the story of a young woman named Arachne. Arachne was the most skilled weaver in the land, a

According to ancient Greek myth, the goddess Athena was so jealous of Arachne's skill as a weaver that she turned the young woman into a spider.

superstar among Greek maidens of the time. Even the gods spoke of her. So marvelous were her creations that the semi-divine nymphs of the forests would come out to watch her work. She could spin the finest fabrics, and she could paint with her threads the most beautiful tapestries. Unfortunately, her reputation was so great—and her pride in her weaving so boundless—that Athena, the goddess of wisdom and the arts, grew jealous. She warned Arachne to be more modest and not to compare her human skills to those of a goddess. Arachne, unafraid and unwilling to hide her talent, would not listen. Instead she boldly challenged Athena to a contest.

Although the goddess and Arachne both wove stunning tapestries, even Athena saw that Arachne's was better. Enraged, the goddess destroyed Arachne's work. The young woman, finally aware of Athena's power and regretful of her own behavior, ran away into the woods. There she wrapped a rope around her neck and started to hang herself. Athena took pity on her and saved her from death. But to teach a lesson to all who think themselves better than a god, she changed Arachne into a spider, fated to hang from her spun silk forever.

Other cultures have also focused on the spider's miraculous skills. Among some Native Americans, Spider Woman was thought of as the creator of the world. From the stuff of the earth, it was said, she created every human being, and she tied each of them to her by a silken thread.

The Navajo tell the story of how the art of weaving was brought to them: Wandering far from her home one day, a young girl saw a thin trail of smoke rising from a hole in the ground. Curious, she went down into the hole and came upon Spider Woman, who had taken the form of an old human. Spider Woman let the girl stay for a few days and taught her how to weave the most marvelous blankets and baskets. The girl

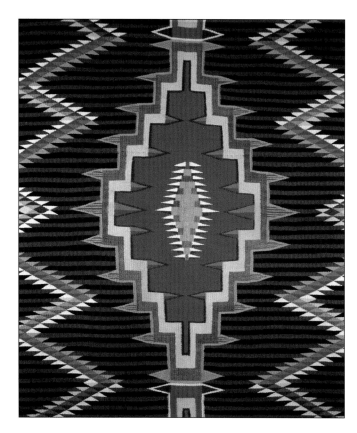

was then allowed to bring this skill back to her people. But she was instructed to tell them that they must always remember to leave a hole at the center of their weaving, or else they would be struck by bad luck. Traditional Navajo crafts to this day are marked by this reminder of Spider Woman's hole in the ground.

On the far side of the world, in West Africa, the spider was woven into many folktales that were later carried by slaves to the Caribbean Islands and the American South. The hero of these stories is Anansi the spider, a clever, manipulating trickster. Anansi stories are similar to stories about Br'er Rabbit (another West African creation). Like Br'er Rabbit, Anansi is not always good or kind or even likable, but he is always admirable. Although he is smaller and less powerful than the other animals, thanks to his cunning, he always manages to come out on top.

In English tales, the spider is rarely so engaging a creature. Still, there is the famous legend of Robert the Bruce, king of Scotland, who in 1306 was defeated in battle by England's King Edward. Weary and discouraged, Bruce lay in a barn, resting. On the ceiling he saw a spider trying to swing from one beam to the next to attach the first line of its web. Six times the spider tried. Six times it fell. But on the seventh attempt, it succeeded. Inspired, Bruce vowed that, like the spider, he too would try again until he

THE WHEEL SPIDER—SO CALLED BECAUSE IT ROLLS LIKE A WHEEL DOWN SAND DUNES TO ESCAPE PREDATORS—IS AT HOME IN THE FORBIDDING NAMIB DESERT OF SOUTHWEST AFRICA.

A BEAUTIFUL ORB WEB DISPLAYS THE "ADMIRABLE" SIDE OF A SPIDER: ITS ABILITY TO WEAVE ASTONISHINGLY COMPLEX CREATIONS OUT OF SILK THREADS.

threw out the invader of his land. His determination paid off. In 1314 he finally defeated England, and he became a hero for generations of patriotic Scots.

In a more modern tale, written by E. B. White, a spider named Charlotte uses her cleverness and her superior spinning skills to save the life of a pig named Wilbur. *Charlotte's Web* has enchanted countless children and parents for half a century. It is among the most beloved spider stories ever told, and Charlotte's fictional death at the end of the book has caused millions of very real tears.

Charlotte is the exception, though. Far more often, the spider is presented as something to be feared rather than loved. American children, encountering a spider, are most likely to behave as Little Miss Muffet did and flee. As it turns out, Miss Muffet may have had good reason to hate having a spider beside her. Miss Patience Muffet was a real person, the daughter of the equally real Dr. Thomas Muffet, who lived in England in the sixteenth century. Dr. Muffet was a strong believer in the

LITTLE MISS MUFFET.

MISS MUFFET, THE NURSERY-RHYME GIRL WHO FEARED SPIDERS, WAS THE REAL DAUGHTER OF A DOCTOR WHO BELIEVED THAT EATING SPIDERS COULD CURE MANY ILLNESSES.

power of spiders to cure nearly any ailment—if the patient swallowed them. Such treatments may well have been too much to bear, even for a daughter named Patience.

Popular culture today generally shares Miss Muffet's attitude. Hollywood has been marching giant, hairy spiders across movie screens for decades: among the more memorable successes are the 1950s' classics *Tarantula* and *Earth vs. the Spider* and 2002's

SPIDER-MAN IS ONE OF THE FEW HOLLYWOOD CREATIONS THAT PRESENT THE GOOD SIDE OF SPIDERLIKE BEHAVIOR. MORE OFTEN, SPIDERS ARE THE VILLAINS OF HORROR MOVIES.

Eight-Legged Freaks. What these films count on is that people naturally find spiders horrifying.

The 1990 horror movie *Arachnophobia* made the connection blatant. Arachnophobia, which means "fear of spiders," is the real name of a psychological problem. People who suffer from it are absolutely paralyzed by the sight of any spider and often by anything even vaguely spiderish. Many psychologists believe that fear is exaggerated by our ignorance of the spider's true nature. If so, then the more we know about spiders and their role in the world, the less likely we are to fear them. Perhaps, like Robert the Bruce, we can grow to admire the "wee beasties"—and the not-so-wee ones as well.

2 How Spiders Developed

Spider Origins

No record exists of the precise debut of spiders on Earth. Like insects, spiders are rather small and soft bodied—soft, at least, compared with rocks—and small, soft creatures are not good candidates for fossils. Their remains are eaten or washed away or ground to dust long before they can become entombed in rocks themselves. All we know is that around 400 million years ago, animals began leaving the sea to seek their fortunes on land. Those animals were ancient arthropods, a name that means "jointed legs." Arthropods make up one of the major groups of the world's animals. Today they include a huge assortment of different creatures, all descendants of those animals that walked ever so bravely onto the land 4 million centuries ago. Among them are all the crabs and lobsters and shrimps in the sea, and all the scorpions, mites, ticks, spiders, and insects on land.

THIS 49-MILLION-YEAR-OLD FOSSIL SPIDER FROM GERMANY IS NOT THAT OLD, IN SPIDER TERMS. SPIDERS STARTED CRAWLING OVER THE EARTH SOME 400 MILLION YEARS AGO.

What they all have in common is that their body is made up of a number of segments and that their flexible legs can assume a great many positions by bending at joints. Those legs allow arthropods to get their body up off the ground, just as ours do. Unlike our mammal body, however—and unlike the bodies of fish and birds and reptiles—an arthropod's body has no bones inside it. It wears its skeleton on the outside. This external support, or exoskeleton, is most easily seen in lobsters or crabs, where it takes the form of a shell. But the design is essentially the same in spiders and insects. In these smaller animals the exoskeleton is a hardened outer covering that both protects the body and holds it together.

Scientists do not know exactly what the spiders' ancestors looked like. The oldest spider fossils discovered are about 330 million years old. By that time, though, there was already a great variety of spiders on Earth, and they were remarkably like the spiders of today. For one thing, they were all predators, animals that hunt other animals for food. Some of them reached impressive size. One spider of 300 million years ago, named *Megarachne servinei*, had a leg span of 20 inches (51 cm). But most were of more familiar size, and then, as now, their main food was insects.

The methods ancient spiders used to catch those insects were less inventive than the methods of today's spiders. Spiders originally used silk as a protective covering for their eggs. Only later did they start to use it in complicated webs and snares. Precisely when is hard to say. Certainly by 130 million years ago, when giant meat-eating dinosaurs were loudly stalking the world, spiders were quietly making insect-trapping webs. Scientists have drawn this conclusion because a strand of silk covered with beads of glue was found encased in a piece of 130-million-year-old amber from Lebanon. Amber is a hard, transparent yellowish stone now, but millions of years ago it was a sticky molasses-like tree sap. Many insects—and a number of spiders—were caught in the sap and stuck for eternity. Today their perfectly preserved bodies are highly prized by scientists for the information they reveal about ancient life.

Spider Relatives

Scientists arrange all living things in groups to show which are close cousins and which are distant relations. The groups are of ever increasing size, and they fit inside one another like a set of dolls. The biggest category is the kingdom. Spiders, like every other animal on Earth, from worm to whale, are part of the kingdom Animalia.

The next broadest category is the phylum (plural, phyla). The phyla separate the animals according to fundamental differences in their body design. All animals with a spinal chord, for example, such as fish, reptiles, birds, and mammals, go into the phylum Chordata. All animals with jointed legs and an exoskeleton, such as spiders and insects, go into the phylum Arthropoda. Arthropod species, by far, outnumber all the other animal species on the planet. Scientists have so far identified about 1.5 million animal species alive today. Roughly three-quarters of them are arthropods.

Within each phylum, animals are further grouped into ever smaller categories of class, order, family, genus, and species. Spiders are assigned to the class Arachnida, named for Arachne, the weaver of Greek myth. In the class with them are all the scorpions, mites, ticks, and daddy longlegs (also called harvest-men). These arachnids are further divided into separate orders. Spiders are in the order Araneae.

The two smallest categories give every type of organism a distinct two-part name: a first name that describes its genus, and

a second that records its species. By tradition, both are written in italics, and the genus name is capitalized. For example, the yellow garden spider is *Argiope aurantia*.

Many people think spiders and other arachnids are insects, but they are not. Insects are off in a class by themselves. The most obvious difference between the two classes is in the number of legs: insects always have six, arachnids always have eight. On those legs, spiders and their arachnid cousins have been traveling an evolutionary road separate from that of the insects for hundreds of millions of years. The result is that, although spiders and insects are closely intertwined in each other's lives, they are very different animals.

What makes a spider a spider? There are a number of features all spiders share. Spiders all spin silk, for one thing, although not all spiders make webs. They also all have pincer-like appendages, called chelicerae, which function as jaws and come equipped with fangs. Nearly all spiders have glands that produce poison, which they inject through their fangs into their prey. Not surprisingly, given such equipment, all spiders are meat eaters—there is not a vegetarian among them. Finally, although all spiders devour meat, none of them can actually swallow solid food. They must all turn their victims into liquid, which they then suck up through their mouths.

Not all spiders are alike, of course. With 38,000 different species, there is bound to be a lot of variety. But all spiders can be gathered into slightly more than a hundred large families. Even more broadly, all spiders can be described as one of two types, on the basis of their eating habits: there are web spinners, who wait for their food to come to them, and there are hunters, who take a more active approach to dining. Another way to divide spiders is by the way they use their deadly fangs. In one group are the true spiders, such as Little Miss Muffet's assailant and Wilbur's savior. In the other group are everyone's favorite blown-up movie monsters: the hairy tarantulas. Both make spectacular use of the body evolution has given them.

A DESERT-DWELLING SCORPION IS NOT A SPIDER, BUT IT IS A RELATIVE. SPIDERS AND SCORPIONS OCCUPY SEPARATE ORDERS IN THE LARGE CLASS OF ANIMALS CALLED ARACHNIDS.

3 The Physical Spider

Spiders may loom quite large in our imagination, but in reality most are quite small. The great majority are just a quarter-inch to a half-inch (6 to 12 mm) long. Most also are an inconspicuous black or brown. But a good number proudly display a hot array of colors, and many are patterned as wildly as any butterfly. These are spiders that people recognize, and so, along with their scientific names, they sport common names that describe their looks: among them are Mexican orangebeauty tarantulas, magnolia green jumpers, zebra jumpers, spotted orbweavers, and whitebanded crab spiders.

A TINY BRIGHT-GREEN CRAB SPIDER INCHES UP A BLADE OF GRASS, ANCHORED BY ITS DRAGLINE. ALTHOUGH WE THINK OF SPIDERS AS LARGE AND DARK-COLORED, MANY ARE QUITE THE OPPOSITE.

Spider Skeleton

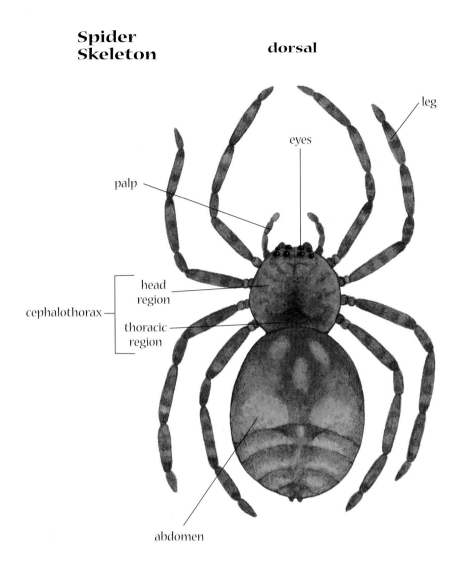

leg

eyes

palp

head region

cephalothorax

thoracic region

abdomen

Whether small or large, plain or gaudy, all spiders boast the same essential body structures. Foremost is the external skeleton, the spider's hard outer support and protection. Without it, a spider would not be able to stand up, let alone crawl or run. An exoskeleton is strong enough to keep the animal safe from

ventral

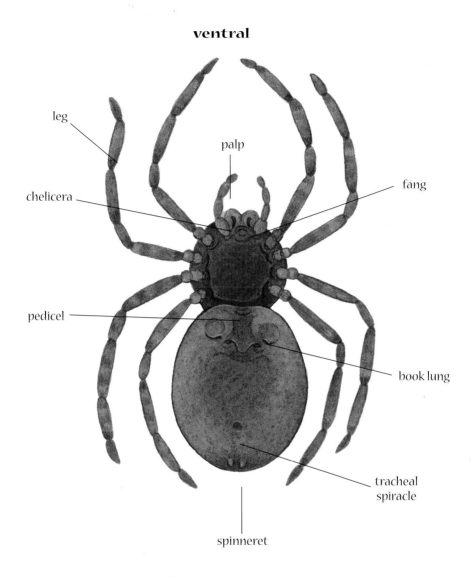

leg

palp

fang

chelicera

pedicel

book lung

tracheal
spiracle

spinneret

many dangers. Its biggest drawback is that, because it is not stretchy, the body inside it cannot grow much. So all arthropods must shed, or molt, their hard skin from time to time. A baby spider, called a spiderling, looks very much like an adult spider except that it is smaller. It will go through as many as ten molts, growing larger each time, in spurts, before eventually reaching adult size.

From the Outside In

Technically, the outer covering of an arthropod is called the cuticle. It is produced by the animal's skin cells, and it consists of several layers. One of the layers is made of a very strong material called chitin, a name that comes from the ancient Greek word for "armor." Chitin is lightweight but hard, and it does an excellent job of protecting the spider while still allowing it to move about. Plates of chitin cover the entire body of the spider, but they are not all of the same thickness. At the joints, where the body needs to bend, the plates are thinner. Where it needs to protect delicate organs, the plates are thicker. The chitin plate over the spider's head, for instance, is especially thick and strong. It is called the carapace, as is the tough shell of a lobster. To keep water out, the outer skin of the spider is covered by a layer of wax. To allow air in, it is perforated in several spots by small tubes.

A spider's body is divided into two segments. An insect, in contrast, has three: a head, a middle segment called a thorax, and an abdomen. A spider's head and thorax are fused, or joined, into a single segment called the cephalothorax (*cephalo* comes from the Greek for "head"). This front-end structure holds all the expected equipment—brain, eyes (a standard eight of them), and assorted mouthparts—plus the four pairs of legs that spiders need for getting those mouthparts from one liquid meal to the next. The abdomen contains such organs as the heart, the intestine, and the reproductive organs, as well as the important glands for producing silk. Linking the cephalothorax and abdomen is a narrowed waist called a pedicel. A pedicel can often distinguish

THE EIGHT WALKING LIMBS OF A DADDY LONGLEGS, OR HARVESTMAN, IDENTIFY IT AS AN ARACHNID, BUT ITS JOINED HEAD AND ABDOMEN SHOW THAT IT IS NOT A SPIDER.

a spider from other arachnids, which generally are not so thin-waisted. Their body segments are either fused into one unit, as in ticks or daddy longlegs, or joined by a much thicker waist, as in scorpions.

Mouth

A spider's mouth is a complex array of different tools, each with a different purpose. Because all spiders are predators, their first essential tool is a weapon that lets them stop and kill their prey. That weapon is a pair of hollow fangs, attached to the chelicerae, or jaws, and connected to poison glands that lie either in the jaws or farther back in the head. Almost all spiders use poison, or venom, to paralyze their prey, but not all spiders are equally powerful. In general, smaller spiders have stronger venom, while the biggest spiders, the tarantulas, rely more on brute force. In a few species—black widow spiders, for one—the venom is potent enough to seriously harm and even kill a human. But most spider bites are harmless or merely annoying to us.

The way the fangs are used divides spiders into two main groups. One is called the araneomorphs (which literally means "spider shaped"), or the true spiders; the other is the mygalomorphs ("mouse shaped") and includes the tarantulas. True spiders have jaws that open out to the sides and fangs that come together horizontally like pincers. Mygalomorph spiders have jaws hinged to the top of the head and fangs that point downward. These fangs work vertically. A tarantula "bites" by raising its fangs high overhead and bringing them down with force—imagine an attack by an eight-legged sabertoothed tiger.

Spiders also use their jaws to crush their victims and make them easier to liquefy. Often the jaws have sharp toothlike points along their inner edge, closest to the head.

Working together with the jaws are two appendages that look very much like legs, except that they are smaller. They are called pedipalps, which means "feeling legs," but they are far more than feelers. The pedipalps, more often just called palps, are

Spider Fang

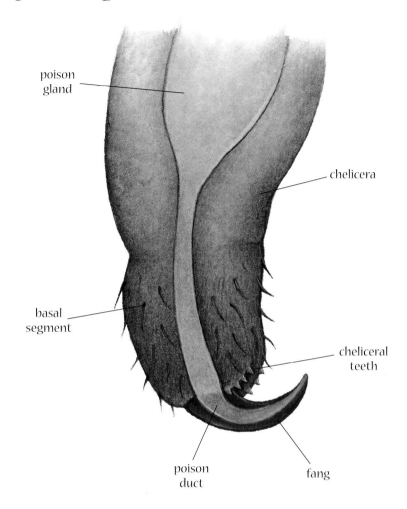

poison
gland

chelicera

basal
segment

cheliceral
teeth

poison
duct

fang

each made of six segments—one less than the seven segments of each leg—and they form the sides of the spider's mouth. Like the jaws, the palps too are often "toothed" on the segment of the palp closest to the body to help crush and grind up prey.

The other attachments on the cephalothorax are the legs, four pairs of them. Going from the body to the tip of the foot, the seven segments of each are coxa, trochanter, femur (equivalent

Spider Leg

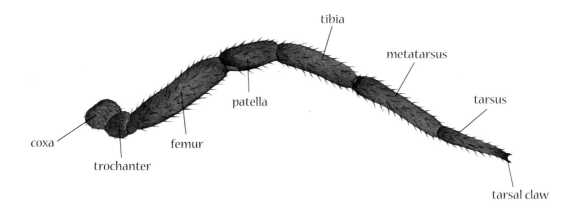

to the human thigh), patella (knee), tibia (shin), metatarsus, and tarsus (foot). At the end of the foot, spiders have at least two claws. Most web-building spiders have a third claw, with which they tightrope-walk over the silken threads of their web. Hunting spiders have a pad of fine hairs, called a scopula, around the bottom of each foot, between the claws. These thousands of tiny hairs, coated with moisture, allow spiders to get a grip on even the smoothest, glassiest surfaces and to walk up walls, across ceilings, and over bathtubs with ease.

Abdomen

The armor shielding the abdomen of a spider is usually not as thick as the covering over the head, so the back part of a spider is normally softer and more flexible than the front. It is also often the most highly decorated part of a spider, splashed with bright colors and patterns. In addition, the abdomen is sometimes adorned with hairs and sharp, thornlike spines, which are outgrowths of the cuticle. An extreme example of this adornment is found on the spinybacked orbweaver from Malaysia (*Gasteracantha arcuata*), whose bright orange abdomen, tattooed with rows of black dots, sports two enormous curved spines sprouting out from its sides like the wings of a handlebar moustache.

Also attached to the abdomen, at the tip, are the spinnerets, the organs the spider uses to spin silk threads. Most spiders have six spinnerets, placed close together, but some species have fewer. Tarantulas, which generally do not depend on silk for bagging their dinner, often have only four spinnerets.

Spinnerets are like short, hollow "fingers." At one end, inside the spider's body, they are connected to glands that produce liquid silk. At the other end, each spinneret is pierced by dozens, and sometimes as many as a hundred, tiny holes, through which the silk flows. The tip of each spinneret is called the spinning field.

The silk does not just ooze out from the spinning field. Spinnerets are very mobile fingers. They can be drawn in and stretched out, and they work together with the back legs to pull the silk out of the body.

One group of spiders also has a flat spinning organ called the cribellum alongside its spinnerets. The cribellum is a super spinning field, with thousands of very small holes, that produces an especially thin and sticky silk. Cribellate spiders combine this sticky silk with other, nonsticky threads to make braided ribbons, called hackled bands, that are terrific at tripping up and ensnaring careless insects.

The last noticeable features on the underside of the abdomen are small openings, called spiracles, that allow air to enter the body and a single opening, called the anus, that allows waste to exit.

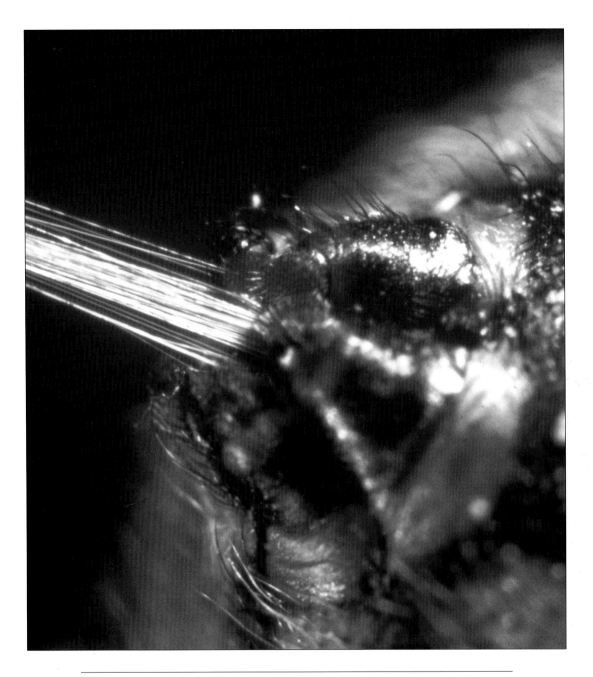

FINE SILK IS PULLED FROM THE SPINNERETS OF A GARDEN SPIDER. THE TIP OF EACH SPINNERET IS PIERCED BY DOZENS OF HOLES, THROUGH WHICH THE SILK EMERGES IN LIQUID FORM.

Legs, Muscles, and Movement

An arthropod's body is built inside out, from a human's point of view. The skeleton is on the outside. Attached to the inside of the skeleton are the muscles. On some spiders, the points where major muscles attach can be seen as small dimples in the surface of the abdomen.

Despite their placement, spiders' muscles are much like our own, and they work the same way. When they contract, or get shorter, they move whatever part of the body they are attached to. Spiders are generally quite strong for their size. They use their powerful muscles to subdue and carry prey, to pull themselves up silken ropes, to walk, run, and even jump. With eight legs, two chelicerae (jaws), two fangs, a pair of palps, and half a dozen spinnerets to keep in motion—not to mention internal organs such as a heart and a stomach—a spider's set of muscles must be reliable and well coordinated.

Spiders are unique, however, in their ability to perform one important movement without any muscles at all. Although, like us, spiders use muscles to bend their legs inward, they have no muscles for extending their legs outward. To stretch out their legs, they raise their blood pressure. The increased force of the fluid inside the hollow legs straightens the kinks right out, just as a rush of water straightens out a garden hose. This kind of system is called a hydraulic system, which simply means it works by the pressure of a fluid, such as water or blood. If there is not enough fluid in a spider's body—if it is bleeding badly for instance, or if it has gone too long without drinking—its legs will fold up, and it will be unable to walk.

This system makes the legs an especially vulnerable part of a spider's body. A leg is often the first part that comes into contact with both predators and prey. Not surprisingly, it is often

From below, the segments that make up this orb-web spider's legs and body are clearly visible, as are the sensitive hairs that cover its skin.

grabbed by an attacking or struggling creature, and sometimes badly mangled. If this happens, a spider simply lets the leg go. It can get by without the leg, but it cannot afford to bleed. So it breaks the leg off close to its body, between the first and second segments. Bleeding at this point stops quickly, and the spider is easily able to scurry off with the rest of its body intact.

When a spider walks, it normally moves four legs at a time: the first and third leg on one side together with the second and fourth leg on the other. But most spiders can function perfectly well without two or three or sometimes even four legs. Besides, a spider can usually regrow a lost limb. So long as a spider has not yet reached its full growth, it will begin to grow a new leg after its next molt. The regrown leg will be shorter than the others, but it will lengthen with each molt until it reaches nearly normal size.

Evidently, losing a leg is not especially tragic if you have eight of them. A spider may even see the loss as a lucky break: often, a spider will retrieve its lost limb and eat it (or more precisely, suck it). No sense in wasting food, after all.

Digestion

A spider must live on a steady liquid diet. Unfortunately, the liquid it needs must come from other animals, chiefly insects, and the world is not filled with insects walking around in liquid form. So the first challenge a spider faces after grabbing an insect is to turn that bug into bug juice.

The solution is predigestion—the spider starts digesting its food before the food enters its body. Once its prey is immobilized, a spider releases strong digestive liquids from glands in the base of its palps. Some spiders bathe their entire prey in digestive juices. Others crunch up the insect first to expose its soft

Spider Organs

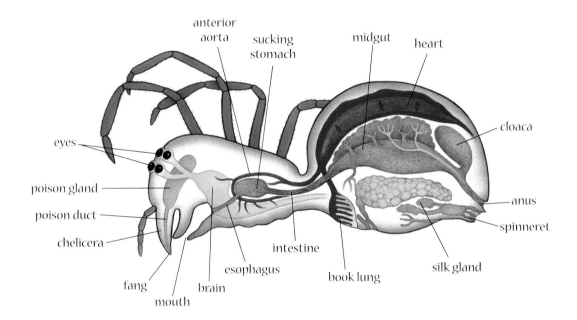

parts. In either case, all that is left after the spider finishes are just the hard outer parts of the insect.

Once the bug has been liquefied, the spider must get it into its body. For this job, it has a strong "sucking stomach," which is housed in the cephalothorax, just behind the brain. Muscles attach the outside walls of the stomach to the inside walls of the exoskeleton. When these muscles contract, they pull on the stomach walls and stretch them so that the stomach gets bigger. The sucking force that is created pulls the liquid food in through the spider's small mouth. The process is similar to what happens when the soft bulb of an eyedropper is squeezed and then released. As the bulb expands, liquid is sucked into the attached tube.

Spiders take extra precautions to make sure that no tiny bits of solid food get in and block up the works. The inside surface of their palps is lined with fine hairs. These hairs work as a filter to trap and remove any bits of food flowing toward the mouth in the stream of liquid food.

Once the food is in the stomach, some of it may be shunted over to little pouches, where it can be stored. Spiders can live off stored food for a remarkably long time. Some longer-lived spiders can go for a year or even a year and a half between meals, if necessary.

The rest of the food is passed through to the abdomen. Muscles that circle the stomach contract and squeeze out whatever is inside. The food travels through the intestine to a part of the digestive tract called the midgut. There the nutrients are absorbed and sent to cells throughout the body. Whatever is not absorbed travels eventually to a chamber called the cloaca, where it is stored as feces until the spider expels it from its body.

Respiration

Spiders, like all animals, need oxygen. But the system they use for getting it is not like our own. We mammals breathe air into lungs. There, red blood cells pick up a load of oxygen, then carry it through a network of ever smaller tubes (arteries and capillaries) to every inch of the body. After shedding its load, the blood returns to the heart through a network of more tubes (veins).

Things work differently in arthropods. Insects, for example, have no lungs, and their blood carries no oxygen. Instead, they have small air tubes, called tracheae, which lead from holes (spiracles) on the outside of the body to the tissues inside.

Spiders have a more complicated system. They have an organ called a book lung, made up of fifteen or more very thin sheets of tissue that are folded up to look like the pages of a book. Air enters through tiny slits on the sides and tip of the abdomen. Oxygen is grabbed by cells flowing through small blood vessels in the book lungs.

Tarantulas and other mygalomorphs have two pairs of book lungs. Most true spiders, which evolved later, have only one pair. The other pair has turned into a system of tracheae and spiracles, like those of insects. Why? Apparently because tracheae are better at delivering oxygen quickly to where it is needed. Mygalomorphs are in fact more sluggish than true spiders. They can move energetically only in brief spurts, and they rapidly run out of breath.

Circulation

To move their blood around, spiders have a simple but effective heart. Basically, it is a tube that runs inside the abdomen, close to the back. Blood collects in the heart and is pumped out through arteries leading to the head and the legs.

Once there, though, the blood does not make a return trip through veinlike tubes. As in insects, the blood spills out the end of the arteries and sloshes around the inside of the spider's body, washing over all the tissues and organs. Eventually it gathers into a pool and passes through one-way valves back into the heart.

This type of circulation is called an open system because the arteries simply open onto the interior of the body. A system like ours, in which the blood is always contained within a network of tubelike blood vessels, is a closed system. If blood does spill out of any of these tubes, something is wrong—somewhere, the animal is bleeding.

Arthropods can bleed, too, and bleed badly. Because their blood is washing in a pool inside their body, any break in their tough skin might allow all the blood to leak out quickly. Bleeding is especially a problem for spiders because they have naturally high blood pressure.

Blood pressure is a measurement of how much force is pushing the blood through the body. Some animals need a lot of force—a giraffe, for example, needs to push blood eight feet (2.4 m) or so from its heart to its brain. Spiders, it turns out, sometimes have a blood pressure higher than that of a giraffe. They need all that force just to keep their legs moving.

Reproduction

Spiders are like most other animals when it comes to the basics of making babies. Females produce eggs in organs called ovaries. Males produce sperm in organs called testes. If a sperm cell merges with an egg cell, the egg is fertilized, and it develops into a new organism.

Brain, Nervous System, and Senses

Despite the inside-out construction of arthropods, they do keep their brain inside their head. The spider is no exception. Its brain is made up of a cluster of nerve cells, called a ganglion, that lie both above and below what would be our throat—the tube leading from mouth to stomach. Nerve fibers run from the brain to all parts of the body. The upper part of the brain receives signals from the eyes and the jaws. The lower part of the brain stays in touch with the legs and the abdomen.

All these parts of the body are constantly sending the brain information about the world they encounter. A spider's senses are well tuned to its surroundings. They have to be. If a spider does not keep close tabs on events and objects around it, it may find that it has become dinner instead of diner.

Spiders look out at the world with eight eyes, so anyone might reasonably assume that they are highly visual creatures. Just the opposite is true. Most spiders, in fact, see very poorly and only at short distances—a couple of inches (5 cm) or less. The great exceptions are the jumping spiders, which hunt down and leap upon their prey. They can see up to about a foot (30 cm) away and are easily the best-sighted spiders in the world. The worst, not counting some blind cave-dwelling species, are generally the web weavers.

The number of eyes a spider has varies by species. Most spiders have eight, lined up in two rows of four, one above the other. Others have six or four or two. In some cave-dwelling species, the eyes have disappeared completely. In a single odd species that lives in the rain forests of Panama, the spider's two eyes have combined into one, making it a terrifying, though tiny, eight-legged cyclops.

Spider eyes are not like the compound eyes of a bee or dragonfly, in which many individual lenses are gathered together into one large eye structure. Rather, spider eyes are simple, each having only a single lens that is formed by the outer skin. These eyes are more like the small additional eyes that many insects have, called ocelli. They are better at detecting movement or patterns of light and shade than they are at forming sharp images. When it comes to keeping things in focus, spiders are far outclassed by their insect prey.

However, spiders more than make up for their lack of good vision by their exceptional sensitivity to touch. A spider's body is

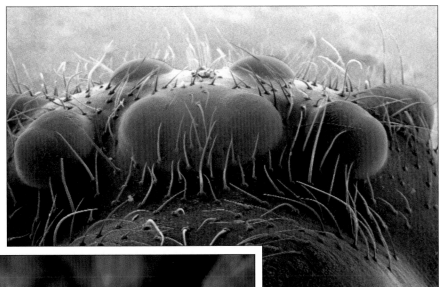

CLOSE UP, THE EYES OF A
BLACK WIDOW SPIDER SEEM
AN IMPRESSIVE ARRAY OF
SENSORS. IN FACT, A BLACK
WIDOW'S SIGHT IS POOR,
AND IT SEES MOTION MORE
THAN CLEAR IMAGES.

TWO OF A WOLF SPIDER'S EIGHT EYES ARE GREATLY
ENLARGED, ALLOWING IT TO SEE BETTER THAN MOST OTHER
SPIDERS. EVEN SO, THE RANGE OF ITS VISION IS ONLY A
FEW INCHES.

covered with touch sensors in the form of very fine hairs, called setae, which pick up any vibrations in the ground or air. Even more sensitive hairs on the legs respond to the slightest movement of air, such as the faint swish of a passing insect's flapping wings. Still other hairs, on the tips of a spider's legs and palps, pick up and taste chemicals they come in contact with. These

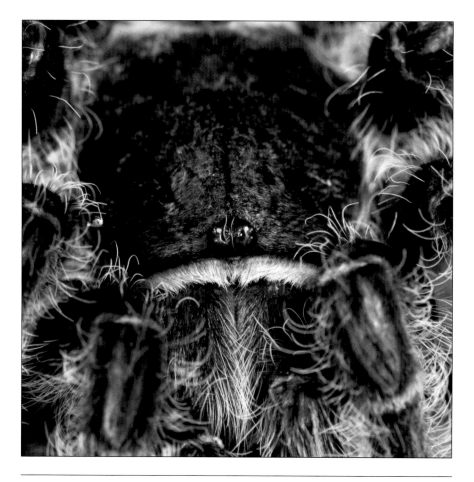

TARANTULAS ARE ESPECIALLY HAIRY SPIDERS—AS NOCTURNAL HUNTERS, THEY RELY ON THE HAIRS' SENSITIVITY TO VIBRATION TO ALERT THEM TO THE APPROACH OF BOTH PREY AND PREDATORS.

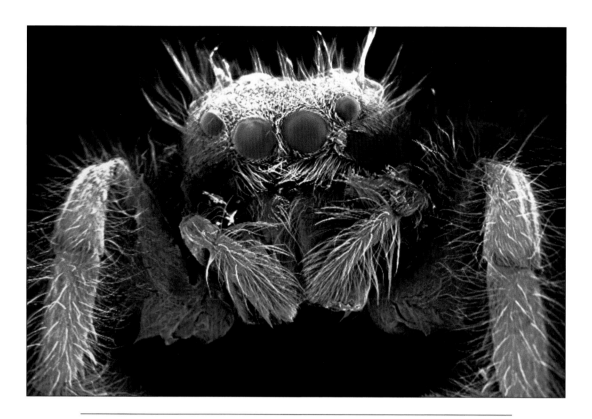

A MICROSCOPE REVEALS A SPIDER'S BLANKET OF SENSORS; SOME HAIRS ON THE LEGS CAN DETECT SLIGHT MOVEMENTS OF AIR, WHILE HAIRS ON THE PALPS CAN SENSE TASTES.

hairs allow the spider to taste any potential food and make sure of its safety before eating it. Spiders do not have ears or a nose. But these arrays of hair sensors allow a spider to smell and to hear and even to see the world in a way that is radically different from anything with which we more vision-dependent animals are familiar.

4 Hunters and Stalkers

Images of spiders usually take one of two forms. The first is a quick, small, shining creature poised in the center of a large, spiraling web—a Halloween picture of a spider. The other is a huge, monstrous, hairy thing, standing solidly on eight thick, horrifying legs—the tarantula, the villain of nightmares and horror movies.

Tarantulas

The name *tarantula* can be confusing. What it means in the United States is different from what it means in Europe. Generally the name refers to any of the really large mygalomorphs (all of which are members of the family Theraphosidae). Tarantulas are the largest spiders in the world, and thanks to their size and their ability to handle large prey, the most dramatic. In tropical forests they are known as bird-eating spiders because

A TARANTULA STRUGGLES TO FREE ITSELF OF ITS OLD SKIN. JUST AFTER
MOLTING, THE NEW SKIN IS VELVETY GRAY AND FLEXIBLE ENOUGH TO
ALLOW THE SPIDER TO GO THROUGH A RAPID GROWTH SPURT.

they occasionally capture small birds, such as hummingbirds. In South America they routinely feed on lizards and frogs and small snakes. According to some reports, they will even attack poisonous snakes by latching on to the snake's head and injecting it with their venom. Nothing the snake can do will shake the spider off; it hangs on tightly until the venom takes effect and the snake stops moving. The tarantula then begins to eat. It may take a full day for the tarantula to devour its meal.

In the United States tarantulas feed mostly on insects such as beetles and grasshoppers. There are some thirty species of tarantulas found here, mostly in the dry regions of the Southwest, although others live in spots stretching from Mississippi to California. Many more live in the deserts of Mexico.

The most noticeable difference between tarantulas and other spiders, aside from their greater size, is their bite: a tarantula's fangs strike downward rather than sideways. To increase the force of its blow or to defend itself, a tarantula will raise itself up on its back legs. Presumably this stance is frightening enough to intimidate an attacker.

It certainly scares many humans. But the tarantula's reputation is far worse than the danger it actually poses. Tarantulas do not kill with a terribly powerful poison. They kill by force. Humans are so much larger than even the largest tarantulas that these creatures cannot do us much harm. A tarantula bite may hurt badly, but it will soon heal. Because tarantulas are so dramatic-looking and because some are beautifully colored, many people keep them as pets. The Mexican redknee tarantula has become such a favorite that its natural population may be threatened.

In the tropics some tarantulas have taken to life in the trees, but in the United States they are all ground dwellers. They dig tunnel-like burrows, often under rocks, where they stay hidden during the day. At night they come out to hunt, but they never go far. Usually they stay within a few yards (a few meters) of their burrow. Tarantulas tend to be true homebodies; they may use the same burrow their whole life—which for these longest lived of all spiders may be a long time. If they can avoid being killed by predators such as skunks or snakes or birds, male tarantulas may live as long as ten years. Females may live twice as long.

A TARANTULA WAITS IN ITS BURROW WITH ONLY ITS FRONT LEGS PROTRUDING. IF PREY COMES WITHIN RANGE, IT WILL MOVE QUICKLY, BUT IT WILL NOT VENTURE FAR FROM ITS HOLE UNLESS FORCED.

Trapdoor Spiders

Trapdoor spiders are very similar to tarantulas. They too are mygalomorphs, although they are members of a different family (Ctenizidae). These spiders spend most of their time—indeed, most of their life—inside tubelike burrows dug into the ground. Sealing off the burrow is a door made of bits of soil glued together with silk and saliva. The entire inside of the burrow is lined with a silken sock, and the door is hinged to the lining.

Most trapdoor spiders are night creatures. When darkness comes, they crawl to the top of their tube, lift the door slightly, and rest their front legs on the ground. In general they have poor

A TRAPDOOR SPIDER OPENING ITS DOOR FROM THE OUTSIDE IS AN UNUSUAL SIGHT. THESE HUNTERS SPEND NEARLY ALL THEIR TIME INSIDE THEIR SILK-LINED BURROWS.

eyesight, and they rely on feeling the vibrations caused by insects walking by. When one comes within reach, the spider grabs it, drags it quickly into the burrow, and lets the door slam shut.

Some trapdoor species leave the safety of their tube for very short attacks. They spin silk trip wires leading out from their hole. When the spider feels a victim tripping over the line, it races out and pounces on it. The door of a trapdoor spider's home is thin and light, designed to pop open as the spider rushes out. When it rushes back in with food, the spider closes the door behind it and dines in peace.

Purse-web Spiders

Closely related to the trapdoor spider is a group known as the purse-web spiders, found throughout the South in the United States. They too live in tubes, which they line with silk. But they continue the silk lining of their burrow above the ground, weaving a hollow sleeve of silk that may be as long as 18 inches (46 cm). Often their burrows are dug at the base of a tree, and the silk tube, or "purse web," runs up the trunk. When an insect lands on the outside of the purse, the spider grabs it from the inside, sinks in its fangs, and drags its victim through.

Not all hunting spiders are mygalomorphs. The real hunters, in fact, are found among the true spiders. These predators are often vagrants, who never establish a home base. They differ in how they go after their prey and how much they use their silk-weaving abilities to capture it.

Jumpers

Among the hunters, jumping spiders are the most spectacular. They are also the best-sighted spiders in existence. Their eyes, arranged in three rows of four, two, and two, can focus sharply up to 12 inches (30 cm) away and can sense movement much farther away than that. The middle two eyes in the bottom row are always large, and people find them engaging. Many human observers feel that jumpers are the one type of spider that actually stares back at them.

Jumpers (all members of the Salticidae family) are all rather small. Most are less than half an inch (12.5 mm). But they can jump as much as forty times their body length, and they put their athletic abilities to good use. Jumpers hunt like cats. They spot

JUMPER SPIDERS STALK THEIR PREY AS CATS DO, USING THEIR LARGE EYES TO TRACK AN INSECT'S MOVEMENTS, THEN LEAPING AS MUCH AS FORTY BODY LENGTHS TO LAND ON TOP OF IT.

their prey visually, and creep up on it, often running a few steps and then freezing. If they are on plants or trees, they may jump from one leaf or branch to another as they home in on their target. When it is finally within range, the jumper uses its pressure-powered legs to leap right onto its victim and then quickly administers a fatal bite.

Jumpers are found around the world in a variety of habitats, from tropical rain forests to the northern United States. They are routinely covered by a brightly colored hairy coat, which often has flashy patterns. One common American jumper (*Salticus scenicus*) sports a black-and-white striped design that has earned it the common name of zebra spider.

Wolves

Wolf spiders (members of the Lycosidae family) also have eight eyes in three rows, with the middle and top pairs, on top of the head, enlarged. These eyes are arranged so that the wolf spider can see forward, upward, and to the sides, and for a spider, it has rather good vision, though not nearly as sharp as a jumper's. At best, a wolf spider can see out to perhaps three inches (7.6 cm) ahead, and it mostly perceives only motion. Still, that vision is good enough for wolf spiders to be skilled hunters. They cannot jump great distances, but they can mount a quick charge and manage a short leap. Most wolf spiders, like the four-footed mammals for which they are named, are quite powerful. Unlike real wolves, however, these spiders never hunt in packs. They are lone wolves.

Wolf spiders range in size from a quarter-inch to an inch and a half (6 to 38 mm). Like jumpers, they are widespread, occupying woods, prairies, gardens, and deserts. Many have an elegant velvety coat of black, brown, or gray. But it is hard to generalize about wolf spiders. Among the hundreds of different species, there are some that hunt in the daytime and some that hunt at night, some that dig burrows and some that live above ground.

Fishers

Fisher spiders are relatives of wolf spiders, but they have a more specialized approach to dining. As their name implies, these spiders (members of the family Pisauridae) prefer to live near water. They are often found along the banks of ponds, lakes, and streams or in the thick of swamps. They do not use silk to catch prey, but they do use the surface of the water much as another spider might use a web.

Typically, a fisher spider will keep its back legs firmly planted on the ground and its two long front legs resting on the surface of the water. When it feels the vibrations caused by a struggling insect that is stuck in the water, it pounces. It will also grab immature insects that develop in water, such as the larvae of dragonflies. If given the opportunity, a fisher spider will happily scoop up small fish as well as tadpoles and small frogs. Some fisher spiders actually lure the fish to them by tapping the water lightly with their legs. The fish, thinking the vibrations are caused by a drowning fly, swim up to the surface for a quick snack. Unfortunately, they become the snack for the spider.

Fisher spiders sometimes use floating leaves or water lilies as hunting platforms. They are also able to run and skim across the surface of the water itself, as the insects called water striders do. On occasion fisher spiders will go underwater to catch prey, but it is difficult for them. Although some can get rather large, the spiders are so light that it is hard for them to break through the water's surface. They must hold on to a leaf or stem

A fisher spider begins to eat a small reed frog. Most of a fisher's diet is made up of insects, but frogs and fish are welcome catches.

on the bank and push hard. To stay underwater, they must find something else to hold on to. Otherwise, air trapped in their hair brings them right back up. Still, some manage to stay under for forty-five minutes or more by breathing that trapped air.

The Water Spider

Diving is not customary behavior, even for fishers. Spiders apparently feel the decision their ancestors made to get out of the water 400 million years ago was a smart one. But one extremely unusual spider ignores that conventional wisdom. The water spider, *Argyronata aquatica*, is the only spider in the world that actually lives underwater. It spends its entire life submerged, hunting, eating, mating, and laying its eggs in a house built of air.

The water spider, found in still lakes and ponds in Europe, is an average-looking small, brown spider about half an inch (13 mm) long. Were it not for its odd lifestyle, we would probably pay no special attention to it. But the life it has devised for itself is remarkable.

Like all spiders, the water spider must breathe air, so it constructs a container to hold air underwater. First it makes a sheet of silk that it attaches to underwater plants so that the sheet is stretched flat and horizontal. Then it swims to the surface and lifts up its hind legs and abdomen. When the spider swims back down, it carries a bubble of air trapped by the hairs on its hind legs and held against its body. It releases the bubble under the silk sheet, which bulges upward and looks like a bell or an overturned cup. The spider repeats this process six or more times, until it has enough air. Then it takes up residence in its bubble home, swimming out at night only to hunt down insects or small water-dwelling creatures or to refresh its air supply.

This home serves the spider well for the warm months of the year. In the winter, the water spider swims deeper and spins a new home, often inside an old snail shell. After filling it with air, the spider seals off the shell and hibernates inside until spring.

Crabs

From their name, one might think that crab spiders too are fond of the water. But these crabs are strictly landlubbers. They resemble real crabs only in that they often walk sideways and that they use their two front legs as pincers.

Crab spiders form a very large group. Some species live on the ground, others in trees, still others on the walls of buildings. A number of them are large, fast runners. But the typical crab spider is small, one-quarter to three-eighths of an inch (6 to 10 mm) long, with a flattened body. Many of these crabs (members of the family Thomasidae) are unlikely hunters. They have poor eyesight and small jaws, and they are slow and ungainly. In fact, many spider specialists classify them as "ambushing" spiders rather than hunters. The favorite hunting strategy of a crab spider is to sit patiently on a flower with its front legs raised a bit and spread open. The spider does not stir until a nectar-loving insect wanders by. When it is within reach, the crab spider closes its forelegs and holds the insect tight until it can inject its poison.

Because its jaws do not open wide, the crab spider has become an expert at aiming its fangs at an especially vulnerable spot. On most insects, the spot is the joint between the head and thorax. A crab spider makes up for its small bite with its powerful venom. It is strong enough to bring down butterflies and moths much larger than itself and even mighty bees. These ambushed meals are caught completely off guard. Many crab spiders have evolved to look very much like the flowers they sit

A CRAB SPIDER WAITS PATIENTLY WITH ITS FRONT LEGS OPEN, READY TO GRAB ANY
FIGWORT-LOVING INSECT THAT COMES WITHIN REACH.

on, and they are well camouflaged. Some have even developed the chameleonlike ability to change color from white to yellow to remain unseen, a patient killer hiding among the blossoms.

Pirates

Pirate spiders do not go out and rob other spiders of their catch. They rob them of their life. Pirates specialize in hunting and devouring other spiders.

Spiders are not especially picky eaters. They will all eat other spiders, even of their own species, when the opportunity presents itself. This is one of the reasons nearly all spiders are loners. It is also why many males are eaten by females after mating. But only the pirate spiders (members of the family Mimetidae) rely on eating other species for the bulk of their diet.

Pirates are crafty—they spin no webs themselves, but they make use of the eating habits of their web-spinning cousins. In a typical attack, a pirate spider will slowly and ever so lightly crawl onto another spider's web. So delicately that the web's owner senses nothing, the pirate cuts a few lines of the web and clears a space for itself. Then, with front legs raised, it tugs on the strands of the web. The occupant, thinking an insect has been snared, rushes over. Neither the pirate nor the web builder can see well; they both respond to touch and vibrations. But the pirate usually responds first. As soon as its victim comes close, the pirate grabs it and quickly sinks its fangs into any available leg. The pirate's poison is very strong, and there is rarely a struggle. Soon nothing is left but an empty web and the dried husk of its departed owner.

5 Web Builders

The classic image of a spider web is grand and circular, built of a dazzling number of artfully laid silken lines. It is a beautiful but deadly trap, glistening with beads of glue that will grasp and hold any insect unlucky enough to blunder into them.

This image is true, as far as it goes. But such a web is built by only one group of spiders. Many, many others build quite different webs. Some are triangles instead of circles, some are a random mess of silk instead of a symmetrical masterpiece. Webs may be laid upon the ground, strung between blades of grass, hung vertically in a tree, or wedged into a corner between ceiling and wall. They may be designed to catch flying insects, hopping insects, or crawling insects. They are all wonderful creations and unique in the animal world.

AN ORB-WEB SPIDER HANGS WITH HEAD DOWN, IN THE CENTER OF ITS VERTICAL WEB, SURROUNDED BY AN AREA OF NONSTICKY SILK THREADS.

Silk Treasures

All spiders use at least a little silk. No spider, for example, ever moves without laying out a dragline attached to something solid—ground, wall, rock, tree, or grass. This line not only helps a poor-sighted spider know where it is but also gives it an escape route. A threatened spider can drop down or scramble up a dragline out of danger. Even spiders that do not spin webs of any kind use silk for lining nests and burrows and for wrapping their eggs.

Scientists have found that spiders possess seven different silk glands. No single spider has all seven, but most have several, and some have five or even six. Each gland produces a different type of silk: some thick, some thin, some stretchy, some sticky, some dry. Some are meant only for wrapping eggs, some for wrapping prey, some for spinning draglines, some for spinning webs. Spiders often combine the types for maximum effect.

Spider silk has been called the strongest natural fiber on Earth. It is several times stronger than a steel wire of the same thickness. It is also among the finest fibers on Earth. The thinnest spider silk is just one millionth of an inch (.00003 mm) thick.

When it comes to making webs, spider silks can be used to fashion a large variety of shapes. The designs, however, fall into a few basic categories: tangled webs, sheet webs, funnel webs, and orb webs. They are arranged more or less by age and complexity. Orb webs are the most complicated and are spun by the most recently evolved web spinners. Tangled webs are the simplest and are spun by spiders that evolved earlier.

Tangled Webs

Tangled webs consist of a jumble of silk lines strung without any apparent order. They are often made by spiders that live in dark

places, such as inside houses or under rocks. The web is not a flat, two-dimensional net. It is a space-filling, three-dimensional maze for unfortunate insects. Generally, these webs are not sticky. They do not need to be. The confusing jungle of lines is enough to snare most prey.

One of the most familiar of the tangled-web weavers is the cellar spider (*Pholcus phalangioides*). This spider (like most of its kin in the family Pholcidae) is often mistaken for a daddy longlegs because its legs are eight times longer than its quarter-inch (6 mm) body. The cellar spider hates to be disturbed and prefers dark, neglected corners of buildings. Its old, jumbled webs, filled with insect remains and dirt and dust, are the cobwebs hated by house cleaners everywhere.

These long-legged weavers have an interesting method of making sure that their prey does not escape their trap. As soon as a cellar spider senses that an insect has entered its web, it immediately starts shaking the web very rapidly to get the sorry insect completely entangled. The spider then goes up to it and wraps it tightly in more silk before eating it.

Also among the tangled-web weavers is a group known as the comb-footed spiders (most of which are members of the family Theridiidae). The name comes from a row of long curved hairs on their back feet. With this "comb" of hair, these spiders pull liquid silk from their spinnerets and throw it over their trapped victim.

One comb-footed spider has a reputation that is far bigger than its half-inch (13 mm) body: the female black widow, one of the small number of spiders whose venom can be deadly to humans. Thanks to its gruesome powers and the small red hour-glass marking on its abdomen, the black widow is among the best known of all spiders and one of the few readily identified by schoolchildren across America.

Comb-footed spiders usually add some architectural flair to their tangled webs. Many weave a flat sheet of silk that serves as a platform from which the spider can hang in the center of its tangle. Many also add lines to anchor the web to supports above and below, such as twigs or stems. Some that prey on flying insects add sticky drops of silk to these vertical lines.

Comb-footed spiders with a taste for ground-dwelling insects, such as beetles or ants, have come up with a clever variety of glue trap. From its web the spider drops lines that it attaches to the ground with glue. However, the lines are not attached too firmly. When an insect bumps into one of the trap lines, it gets tangled and starts to struggle. In struggling, it breaks the line free from the weak glue attachment. The springy silk line immediately yanks the insect up off the ground. With its legs in the air it is helpless. With the approach of the spider, it is dead.

Sheet Webs

Silk sheets are a luxury for most humans. For spiders they are extremely common. Many spiders construct their webs out of a flat, two-dimensional sheet of intersecting silk lines. The webs are usually strung horizontally. They may be close to the ground, on grass blades, or some distance above it, in bushes or small trees. Above this sheet the spider builds a vertical maze of criss-crossing threads. A flying or hopping insect gets clipped by one of the upright lines, stops dead in its tracks, and drops to the sheet below. The spider, hanging below the sheet, runs to the spot where the insect fell, bites a leg sticking through the web, then pulls the insect through and wraps it tight. Afterward the spider repairs its web and waits for its next meal to drop from the sky.

Some sheet webs are as large as a foot (30 cm) or more across. Others are quite tiny, less than an inch (25 mm) across. Commonly, many hundreds or thousands of these webs can be seen together in a dewy meadow or garden. They testify to the number of spiders living there, each content to keep within the bounds of its soft dining table.

Many of the sheet-web builders are themselves quite tiny, smaller than the head of a pin. Among them are the little black spiders that in England are known as money spiders (members of the family Linyphiidae); according to superstition, people who find one of these tiny spiders crawling on them will soon be rewarded with treasure. By hanging beneath their horizontal web, these spiders are hidden and protected from predators above them. Some sheet-web builders also spin a second sheet, to protect them from predators below them.

Funnels

A number of spiders have taken the basic sheet-web design and added a cozy hideaway for themselves: a funnel-shaped structure that is attached to the main sheet, either at the center or at an end. Often the funnel is stretched out along the ground or just above it. But it may also be hidden within a bush or among tall plants. Like other sheet webs, the funnel web often has a vertical maze of lines running above the sheet to intercept passing flies or grasshoppers. The spider's funnel home is below the sheet. There it sits and waits, hidden from both predators and prey. When the spider feels a disturbance in the web, it rushes out to grab its catch. Then it drags its meal back into the funnel to eat.

The funnel is open at both ends so that in an emergency the spider can escape. Even so, the spider may well spend its whole life in this same web. Like any proud homeowner, it quickly repairs any damage. It also continually improves and adds to its web, the additions making the web thicker and broader as time goes by.

Orb Webs

Orb webs are the standard symbol of the spider. Many people think these large, spiraling, symmetrical structures are among

ITS PREY KILLED, A FUNNEL WEB SPIDER PREPARES TO DRAG THE MEAL INTO THE FUNNEL-SHAPED HIDEAWAY THAT IT HAS ADDED ONTO ITS HORIZONTAL SHEET WEB.

the most beautiful of nature's creations. No doubt it is the spider's surprising ability to weave such complex designs that led to its reputation for cleverness.

In fact, spiders operate by instinct, not thought. They are "programmed" to make the kinds of web they make, and they are able to do so as soon as they come into the world.

Still, just because a spider does not have to think about what it is doing does not make its achievement any less remarkable. Orb webs are superbly designed for their purpose. These webs are aimed at flying insects, and they are generally hung vertically from trees or bushes. They are lightweight, strong but stretchy, nearly invisible even in daylight, and unaffected by water. As an insect trap, they are unbeatable, and they provide their builders with a steady supply of food, day and night. They can support a spider many times the weight of the web itself—after the mygalomorphs, the largest spiders are orb-web builders. Orb webs are also, for all their complexity, easily rebuilt. The typical orb web takes about an hour to construct, and many spiders build a new web every day.

The number of different spider species that spin orb webs is very large (most are members of the family Araneidae), and they are found around the world. The biggest of them are known as silk spiders (belonging to the genus *Nephilia*), and they cover the trees of tropical forests with immense webs. Silk spiders can be as large as two inches (5 cm), with a leg span four times that. Their beautiful orb webs are often more than three feet (9 m) across and are strong enough to capture a small bird. The only silk spider in the United States is the golden silk orb-weaver (*Nephila clavipes*). It is only half as large as its tropical cousin, but its web is no less spectacular.

Although we see orb webs as beautiful, the spider does not. In fact the spider, with its poor vision, never sees the whole of its web at all, at least not as we do. It builds and operates the web almost totally through its sense of touch.

Orb webs come in a great many more designs than do other spider-silk creations. But they share some common features and are built in similar ways. Typically, the orb-web spider begins its web with a "bridge line," a silk strand strung horizontally from, say, one branch or twig to another. There are two ways for the spider to string this first, critical line. The first is to attach a line to one spot, then walk it over to another attachment point. As the spider moves, it must constantly spin out silk, and it must keep the line from getting tangled as it climbs down and up trunks and stems and over whatever stands in its way. The other method of stringing the bridge line is for the spider to spin a long, fine thread and just let a breeze carry it out until it snags on something. When the spider, by tugging, feels that the line is secure, it attaches the first point.

The bridge line is the most important part of the web, because everything else is hung from it. So the spider's first job is to walk across the newly strung line from end to end, spinning out a new, much thicker silk as it goes. The spider may attach the original thin line to this new thread for extra strength, or it may eat it—spiders recycle their silk.

Once the bridge is strong and tight, the spider reverses direction and again walks the line from end to end, this time spinning a loose, droopy line that hangs down below the bridge. The spider attaches this droopy line, but does not pull it taut. Like a tightrope walker, the spider makes its way along the loose line back to a spot in the middle. It attaches a new thread to this center spot. Then it drops straight down until it touches something—the ground, say, or another branch. The spider pulls the line tight and anchors it firmly.

The result is that the loose line dangling under the bridge is pulled down in the middle so that it forms the top of a Y. The vertical line forms the bottom of the Y. The spot where they meet will be the center of the web. Each of the three lines of the Y now becomes a radius of the circular web—a line that runs from the center to the outside edge, like the spoke of a bicycle wheel. The bridge becomes the first frame line of the web—a line that goes around the perimeter.

Web Building

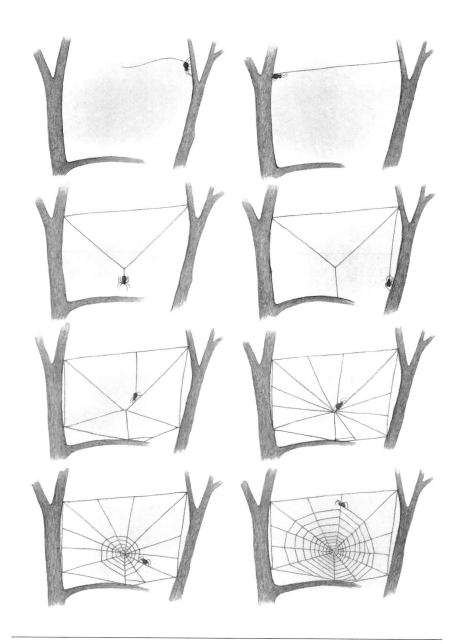

ONE OF THE COMMON FEATURES OF AN ORB WEB IS A BRIDGE LINE. A LOOSE LINE DANGLES UNDER THE BRIDGE AND THEN IS TIGHTENED TO FORM THE TOP OF A Y.

The busy spider now climbs back up to the bridge. From each end it starts laying down more frame lines, building the borders of the web along the sides and bottom. Once these lines are in place, the spider adds more radial lines (spokes) from the frame to the center. The number of radial lines it adds depends on the size of the web, which in turn usually varies with the size of the spider. The spider figures out where it needs another radial line by sitting in the center of the web and feeling around with its legs. If it senses too much space, it adds a line. In the end, a web may have as many as fifty radial lines.

When all these lines are set, the spider lays down a dense circle of threads in the center. This platform will be the hub of the web. From the hub, the spider now walks in a spiral out toward the frame, stepping from one radial line to the next. As it walks, it spins a long, continuous silk thread, which it attaches to each of the radial lines. This is a temporary spiral, put down to keep the web stable. It will soon be replaced.

As the spider spirals outward, the space between radial lines gets larger, and the spider must take bigger and bigger steps. When it feels that the space is too large to cross, it stops. It is time for the last, crucial addition to the web: the trap line.

To this point, all the silk the spider has put into its web has been dry and nonsticky. The silk it now starts to spin is different. It is a combined thread, made of two dry lines twined together and coated with a thin layer of sticky liquid silk. As the spider now works its way back along the temporary spiral toward the center of the web, it lays down a new, more closely spaced spiral of this sticky thread, attaching it to each radial line it passes. (The spider often eats the temporary spiral as it goes.) Each time the spider glues the new thread to a radial line, it stops and gives the sticky thread a quick snap. The snap tightens the line. It also causes the sticky liquid coating to break up into little dots of glue, which now adorn the line like beads on a necklace.

At some point before it reaches the center, the spider stops spinning the trap line. It always leaves a clear, nonsticky area surrounding the hub. Different spiders treat the hub in different ways. Some cut it out. Others decorate it with thick white zigzagging bands whose function is not clear. Originally, scientists thought these bands helped stabilize the web, and so they named them stabilimenta. However, experiments have suggested that the bands may serve other purposes. They may, for example, make the web more visible to birds and so keep them from flying into and destroying it. It is also possible that they help attract insect prey. These zigzagging bands of silk nicely reflect ultraviolet light, a form of light humans cannot see but insects can. Many flowers have patterns that are revealed only by ultraviolet light, and the bands may trick an insect into mistaking the web for a nectar-rich blossom.

With the orb web finished, the spider has nothing to do but wait. Many spiders hang in the center of the web, always head down, their front legs touching the radial lines to feel the vibrations of any visitor. Others prefer to wait offstage, retreating to a spot slightly away from the web—perhaps to the shelter of some curled-up silk-lined leaves. These spiders stay in touch with their web by holding on to a line attached to its center.

In either case, the spider will be alert to any tremor let loose by a suddenly trapped insect. In a flash the spider will be on top of its victim. After touching and tasting it and finding it safe to eat, the spider will quickly wrap its tasty morsel in silk and subdue it. (Many spiders wrap their meal like a mummy before eating it. Sometimes they do it before the insect is paralyzed, to keep from being injured by flailing legs and jaws. Often they will also wrap up an already motionless insect, the object being to keep their food in one leakproof container once it is turned to liquid.)

One of the most obvious but interesting questions about spiders is, Why do they not get stuck in their own webs? The answer lies in their feet and their navigation skills. Web spiders have a third, curved claw on each foot, which acts as a hook. When a spider walks on a web, it grasps the line between this claw and a small rake of hairs that line the leg. The claw glides over the dry, nonsticky silk of the radial lines—the only lines the

A SPIDER OFTEN WRAPS ITS PREY IN SILK—NOT TO KEEP IT FROM ESCAPING BUT TO KEEP IT FROM DRIBBLING AWAY AS INJECTED DIGESTIVE FLUIDS TURN THE PREY INTO LIQUID.

spider travels on. That is why it is important that it does not place the radial lines too far apart. For extra protection, spiders are coated with a layer of oil that helps keep their glue from sticking to them. Still, a spider is careful around its web. It always hangs by its feet, keeping its body away from its own sticky snares.

Web Casters and Ogres

Finally, some groups of spiders are neither quite web builders nor silk-shunning hunters. These spiders have a foot (or four) in both camps. They make marvelous use of their silk-spinning abilities, but they are not content to sit back and wait for their food to come to them. They actively hunt with silken snares, and they do so in devious ways.

The kindest name given to members of the genus *Dinopis* is web-casting spiders. Less kind but equally appropriate names include stick spider and ogre-faced spider. (The genus name itself is not quite as bad as it may sound; it comes from the Greek meaning "terrible appearance.") The ogre-faced stick spider's long drawn out body is generally colored a mottled brown or gray, and by day, it blends in well with the branches and twigs around it. It enhances its camouflage by staying very still, looking for all the world like a motionless stick. On its head the spider has two enormous eyes that, coming as they do at the end of a stick, give it a monstrous appearance.

At sunset the spider begins its preparations for a night's hunt. First it spins a small square sheet of very sticky silk, about the size of a postage stamp. Holding the sheet in its front legs, the spider hangs head down from its perch on a tree or bush and lowers itself on a dragline. Then, still upside down, it waits, its silk snare held taut at the corners by four legs.

Sooner or later the spider's patience will be rewarded. A

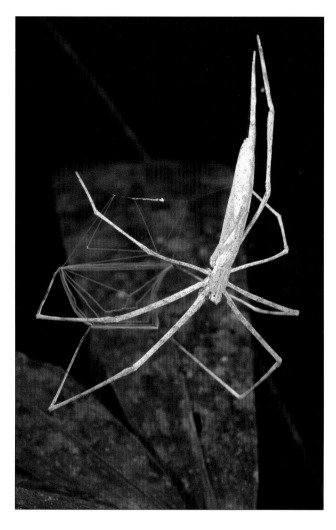

DANGLING UPSIDE
DOWN AT THE END
OF ITS DRAGLINE, A
NOCTURNAL STICK
SPIDER PREPARES TO
TOSS ITS SMALL,
STICKY NET OVER A
PASSING INSECT. (THE
NET IS COLORED BLUE
TO MAKE IT VISIBLE.)

beetle or other insect will come trundling by, unaware of the danger hanging above. When it is directly underneath, the spider will stretch out its forelegs, swoop down, and scoop up the insect in a silken straitjacket. With its prey unable to move, the ogre can dine at its leisure.

Some stick spiders catch flying insects as well. Whether they rely on vision to bag the bug is not clear. Somehow the spider senses when a mosquito, say, or a moth is near. Then quickly it stretches out its legs and holds the sticky web right in the insect's flight path. Even an acrobatic mosquito cannot change course fast enough to avoid capture.

Bolas

Even more surprising are the hunting habits of the cowboylike bolas spiders. These members of the genus *Mastophora* can easily compete with the ogres in any arachnid beauty contest. Bolas are usually round, fat, wrinkled, and short—no more than half an inch (13 mm) long. They are decorated with an assortment of spines, horns, bumps, and lumps. Luckily, they do not need to count on their looks to win them a meal.

Bolas spiders take their name from the twirling ball-and-rope "lasso" of South American cowboys. Their targets, though, are usually moths rather than cattle, and, relatively speaking, a moth is a lot harder to bring down.

Bolas are nighttime hunters. At dusk, they prepare for action by attaching both ends of a silk line to a branch so that the line hangs down like a trapeze. The spider climbs onto the trapeze and spins another line, a rope on the end of which it attaches a bead of very sticky silk. The spider transfers the rope from its spinnerets to its front legs, hangs upside down or sideways from its trapeze, and waits for a moth to fly within range. When the moth comes, the spider swings toward it and at the same time flings out the sticky end of its rope. If its aim is true, the glob at the end of the rope glues itself to the moth, which is stopped dead in its flight.

Spider researchers have long admired the bolas's hunting skills, but only recently did they really appreciate just how remarkable these spiders are. In 2002 scientists proved what

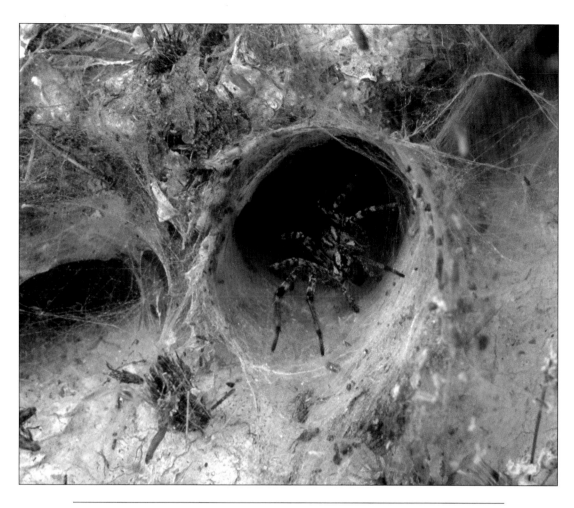

A FUNNEL-WEB WEAVER HIDES NEAR THE FRONT ENTRANCE TO ITS FUNNEL, NEXT TO
ITS SHEET WEB. THERE IS A REAR OPENING ALSO, IN CASE THE SPIDER NEEDS TO MAKE
A HASTY ESCAPE.

they had long suspected: the spiders do not just wait patiently
for a moth to fly close enough to be lassoed; they actually lure
the moth into their trap. Bolas spiders, it turns out, produce
chemicals that mimic moths' pheromones (scents that the
female moths use to attract males). Male moths are exquisitely

sensitive to these scents and will follow even the faintest whiff for long distances, unaware that a spider may lie at the end of the trail.

Spitters

Spitting spiders do precisely what their name promises. The skillful hunters have turned the venom-producing glands in their head into glue factories, and by spitting on their prey, they nail it to the spot.

A FEMALE SPIDER WRAPS HER EGGS IN A PROTECTIVE SAC, WHICH SHE HAS ATTACHED TO NEARBY TWIGS. THE SILK IN THE EGG SAC IS ONE OF SEVEN DIFFERENT KINDS SPUN BY SPIDERS.

Spitting spiders (members of the family Scytodidae) are found around the world. In the United States they have taken up residence inside many homes, although the humans in those homes are probably unaware of their arachnid housemates' dining practices. One of the American species, *Scytodes thoracica*, is fairly typical of the group: less than half an inch (13 mm), with long legs, a yellow body marked with black dots and stripes, and a very rounded, domed cephalothorax. Its hunting method is also typical of its kind. When prey comes within spitting distance—about a quarter inch to half an inch (6 to 13 mm) away—the spider quickly turns to face it. The spitter's body then gives a spastic shudder, and from its jaws spews forth a stream of deadly gum. As it shoots out its glue, the spider rapidly swings its jaws back and forth so that the glue comes out in a zigzag pattern and covers a wide area. The attacked insect has very little chance of escape. The spitting spider has only to come up carefully and give it a quick injection.

6 Life Cycle

Spiders live as loners, but they generally start out with lots of company. Spider eggs hatch within a specially prepared silken container called an egg sac. The smallest spiders may deposit only two or three eggs in the sac, but most spiders lay many more. On average, a spider begins its life with around a hundred siblings. But the larger the spider, the greater the number of eggs. Tarantulas routinely deposit 1,000 eggs in a spherical egg sac measuring 2 to 3 inches (5 to 7.5 cm) across.

Courting and Mating

After mating, males generally disappear, often through no action of their own. A fair number of male spiders get eaten by the female they had so recently been courting. Many people incorrectly believe that all male spiders meet this fate. But in some species, the male simply walks off after mating, and in several,

A GREEN LYNX SPIDER LIES ON TOP OF ITS EGG SAC, GUARDING IT FROM PREDATORS. THE FEMALE LYNX, NORMALLY A MOBILE HUNTER, WILL STAY WITH ITS EGGS UNTIL THEY HATCH.

the male and female share the same web for a while. For many males, however, becoming a mate's meal is a very real danger. Female black widows do indeed often eat their mate (the reason they are called widows), although some males manage to escape.

This practice is not as sinister as it sounds. Many males do not live long after mating anyway, and the extra nutrition a spider's body gives to its mate will benefit the offspring. Still, male spiders need to mate *before* being devoured. To avoid meeting death too early, they have evolved some elaborate mating rituals.

These rituals vary enormously, but they can be broadly grouped into those used by hunters with good vision, those used by hunters with poor vision, and those used by spiders that spend their time sitting in webs.

Wolf spiders and jumping spiders, which have the best eyesight, rely the most on visual clues. These males are routinely colored with bright patches of hair on their "knees" or palps, or with strikingly bold black and white stripes. Their colors can be dramatic: brilliant reds, purples, oranges, and yellows, and sometimes metallic greens and blues as showy as those on the coat of a dragonfly. A mature male jumper will go in search of a female, proudly strutting his colorful stuff. When he finds one, he will immediately start displaying his wares by dancing. Facing the female, he will raise, wave, and wiggle his palps and front legs, holding them out to the sides, then above his head. To us, it looks very much like a sailor sending a message with semaphore flags. With luck, the female is able to read the code.

Such adornment would be wasted on poor-sighted, night-hunting trapdoor spiders and tarantulas. For them, the essential message from male to female must be transmitted by senses other than sight.

Females among these spiders probably advertise their availability through pheromones. But once a male arrives, he must climb into the female's burrow without provoking her to attack. Using touch, he tries to get her to relax her guard. As soon as he makes contact with a female, he starts tapping out a rhythm on her body with his front legs. Then he begins gently stroking her. Most often, these gestures are enough to communicate the male's intentions. If they are not, and the female attacks him, at least he has a chance. Among these spiders males and females do not differ that much in size.

For the web builders, it is a much different story. These spiders also have poor vision, but the males tend to be much smaller than the females. If they do not get their message across, they are doomed. So web-dwelling males start communicating at a distance. When a male finds a female's web—which he probably

THIS SOUTH AFRICAN WOLF SPIDER SHOWS OFF ITS LUXURIOUS RED PALPS, WHICH ARE THOUGHT TO MAKE THE SPIDER APPEAR ESPECIALLY HANDSOME TO FEMALES.

recognizes by distinctive chemicals he can taste in her silk—he begins tapping or plucking at the strands. The web is built, of course, so that any vibration will be instantly felt and recognized by its owner. Normally the vibrations will be caused by the frantic struggles of a trapped insect. The male spider's vibrations are different—regular and rhythmic. If the male is eloquent, the female will allow him to come onto the web.

Preparing for Birth

Many female spiders are finished with motherly duties once they seal their eggs inside the sac. They leave the sac on the ground or attached to leaves or twigs or under the bark of a tree. Others watch over the sac for weeks, until the eggs hatch. Burrowing spiders usually attach the sac to the lining of their burrow. Orb-web spiders either place the sac in the web itself—often right in the middle—or else wrap it inside a nearby leaf. Long-legged cellar spiders are not comfortable leaving their eggs anywhere. They carry the sac with them, in their jaws. Some wolf spiders, also caring mothers, keep the sac attached to their spinnerets.

When the eggs hatch, the spiderlings are not yet fully developed. They must stay inside their temporary silk home until they go through their first molt. By the time they have shed that early skin and grown a bit, they are ready for the world. Most spiders are able to bite their way out of the egg sac. In a few species, though, the mother must help them.

Young Spiders

The spiderlings' behavior on emerging from the egg sac depends on their species. Most spiderlings very quickly go their own separate ways, and for good reason. Even young spiders do not let family ties stand in the way of a needed meal. If food becomes scarce, as can happen with too many hungry spiderlings in one spot, they will eat each other.

A number of species at least postpone this dark state of affairs. Trapdoor spiders and tarantulas keep their young in their burrow for a while after they hatch. There they watch over the spiderlings until they are ready to strike out on their own. Nursery web spiders weave a silk tent to house and protect the spiderlings after they emerge from the egg sac. The mother sits by the opening to the tent and guards the spiderlings against any intruder. Some wolf spiders take their babies with them when they go hunting. After the mother helps the spiderlings get out of the egg sac, they climb up onto her back and ride with her as she searches for food. They stay atop her, each tethered by its own dragline, until they molt a second time. Only then do they wander off.

Large burrowing spiders, when it is time to move away from home, simply walk until they find a suitable location. The distance they travel may be short—many burrowers live their entire life within a few feet of their birthplace, and so unclaimed territory may be nearby.

The smaller web spiders, though, have developed a unique method for spreading themselves out. Once they leave the egg sac, the spiderlings seek out new homes by casting themselves on the wind. The process is called ballooning, and it is as close as spiders ever get to the flying lifestyle of their distant insect relations.

Ballooning is made possible by the spiderlings' clever use of their silk. As soon as they sense that conditions are right, the spiderlings climb to the top of tall grass blades or shrubs or fence posts—whatever vertical structure is convenient. They turn to face the wind, tilt their little abdomens upward, and let the

SPIDERS OFTEN HATCH WITH DOZENS OF SIBLINGS, BUT THEIR TIME TOGETHER IS VERY BRIEF. THEY MUST DISPERSE QUICKLY, BEFORE THEY BEGIN TO REGARD ONE ANOTHER AS FOOD.

breeze pull out a thin line of silk from their spinnerets. When the pull on the silk is strong enough, the spiderlings let go of their hold on Earth and are carried aloft. If they are unsuccessful, they will spin out new silk lines and try again and again.

Some spiderlings flip around to grab the silk line with their legs as they fly. Apparently, they can control their flight somewhat by lengthening or shortening the line. For the most part, though, the spiderlings are carried wherever the wind and air currents take them. Many travel fairly low—200 feet (60 m) or lower. But a great many are carried as high as 5,000 or even 10,000 feet (1,500 to 3,000 m), and they can travel hundreds of miles.

Spiders are born throughout the warm-weather months, but most arrive in the spring and fall. At certain times of the year, thousands upon thousands of spiderlings are ballooning simultaneously, and their silk threads fill the air. In some areas local wind conditions conspire to bring a great many of these threads together in one spot, and silken sheets can be seen covering meadows and trees. These windblown silks are called gossamer. They are the remnants of perhaps millions of attempts by tiny spiders to get themselves airborne.

Many of the spiderlings, unfortunately, will be dropped in inhospitable spots, such as oceans or lakes, where they will die. Many, many others will be killed by predators. Most spiderlings, in fact, do not survive to maturity.

Growing Up

Those that do survive will spend the next part of their life hunting and feeding and growing in spurts. They will go through a number of molts—from three to ten, depending on size, though a long-lived tarantula may molt twenty times before it dies. Many

A FEMALE WOLF SPIDER IS AMONG THE MOST DILIGENT OF SPIDER MOTHERS,
CARRYING HER NEWLY HATCHED OFFSPRING ON HER BACK WHILE SHE GOES HUNTING
FOR FOOD.

spiders do not become sexually mature and able to reproduce
until after the last molt. Before that time, it is nearly impossible
to tell the males from the females. Only at maturity do the sexes
begin to look different. Males may be more brightly colored, for
example, or grow larger palps.

In many species, though, there is a significant difference in size between males and females, even before maturity. Such a difference between the sexes, called sexual dimorphism, is most noticeable among the orb-web spiders. Many of these male spiders are only one-quarter to one-eighth the size of the females. The most extreme examples are the giant silk spiders (*Nephilia*) of the tropics. Among these spiders, the females may be one hundred times the size of the males.

There are some good reasons for the inequality. Females must produce and nurture the eggs, and so they need a larger body. In addition, more bulk is obviously helpful for those spider females who guard their egg sac or give some care to the emerging spiderlings. Males, on the other hand, are not needed after they have completed their role in mating. There is no need to waste energy on building a bigger male body. Males, in fact, routinely die not long after mating.

For most female spiders, the construction of the egg sac is the point, and the final act, of their life. Their entire journey, from birth to death, lasts no more than a year. Several types of spiders do have longer life spans. Wolf spiders may live two years or more; purse web and trapdoor spiders may stick around for seven. But the record for spider longevity goes to the tarantulas. These hairy mygalomorphs may live for a whopping 25 years, secure in their silk-lined underground homes—if nothing cuts their lives short.

Dangers and Enemies

Even a mighty tarantula cannot always escape the dangers that threaten a spider's life. All spiders are on constant guard against a host of deadly enemies that range in size from microscopic fungi to giant humans. In between are such active spider eaters

THREATENED, A TARANTULA RAISES ITS FRONT LEGS AND PALPS AND BARES ITS FANGS,
SIGNALING THAT IT IS READY TO FIGHT IF NECESSARY.

as birds, snakes, skunks, shrews, and other arthropod-loving animals. There is also the threat posed by other spiders, which will
often dine on spider eggs, spiderlings, and adult neighbors. But
the most deadly enemy of these fearsome insect eaters are the
insects themselves.

Certain species of flies and wasps kill a huge number of
spiders every year. They prey on spiders not to feed themselves
but to feed their offspring. These insects are parasites, living off
the bodies of others. For their purposes, spiders are an ideal
food source.

The wasps are the worst. Some of the so-called spider wasps (members of the insect family Pompilidae) sting the spider so that it cannot move and lay an egg on its abdomen. The spider lives, but it is gradually eaten from the inside by the developing wasp larva. Other wasps paralyze the spider and bury it together with their eggs. Among these wasps are several species that specialize in tarantulas. Others prefer smaller web builders.

A FEMALE POMPILID WASP HAS SUBDUED A TARANTULA WITH A WELL-PLACED STING. THE TARANTULA, ALIVE BUT PARALYZED, WILL SERVE AS FOOD FOR THE WASP'S DEVELOPING OFFSPRING.

Defenses

Although spiders are strong, heavily armored, and venomous, they do not like to fight. When faced with danger, spiders are more likely to run away or hide. Trapdoor spiders, for example, often dig side tunnels in their burrows, each equipped with its own door. If an invader enters the burrow, the spider will race into the side tunnel and hold the door closed. The outside of the door is covered in silk and dirt and is hard to see. With luck, the invader will think the burrow is empty.

One trapdoor spider (*Cyclocosmia truncate*) has developed a bizarre body shape to achieve an empty-burrow illusion. The spider's abdomen is cone-shaped and tapers outward. The end of its abdomen is circular but flat and covered with a tough, leathery, crinkled skin. This spider digs a burrow that goes straight down, with tapering sides. If endangered, the spider dives to the bottom of its burrow, head first. Its abdomen becomes a perfectly fitting plug, and its flat rear end looks convincingly like the dirt floor of the burrow. Any invader will take one look at the burrow and decide that no one is home. At least, that is the way things are supposed to work. Wasps are not always fooled.

When threatened, tarantulas will assume a defensive stance, rearing up on their hind legs and baring their fangs. They will also use their rear legs to scrape hairs off their abdomen. These hairs are quite irritating to the eyes and nose of any mammal (including a human), and a small burning cloud of them is often enough to make a predator change his dining plans.

In general, though, spiders would rather not be noticed and attacked in the first place. Many ambushing crab spiders, for instance, have taken on the color and markings of the flowers they most prefer to sit on. Others have gradually adopted the

A BRIGHT-YELLOW CRAB SPIDER BECOMES A MEAL FOR AN ASSASSIN BUG. APPARENTLY THE SPIDER'S CAMOUFLAGE COLORING WAS NOT ENOUGH TO FOOL ITS PREDATOR.

color and texture of bark. A few have gone so far as to look exactly like fresh bird droppings. As it happens, bird droppings are avoided by animals that eat spiders. But they are attractive to insects on which spiders feed. In a world of eat or be eaten, it pays to know who finds you delectable.

7 Spiders and People

Uses and Abuses

Human attitudes toward spiders have changed in the past few centuries, though not necessarily for the better. Back in Little Miss Muffet's day, people often saw spiders as having some beneficial use. Many people, like Dr. Muffet, believed that spiders could cure ailments ranging from warts to fevers to leprosy. Doctors instructed patients to wear spiders around their neck, rub spider ointment on their skin, drink spider brews, and swallow spiders whole and powdered, alive and dead. (None of these measures worked. The one remedy that may have had some effect was applying a spider web to a wound to stop the bleeding. The silk probably did help the blood clot, but since spider webs are hardly sterile, they probably caused a lot of infections as well.)

IN CAMBODIA, TARANTULAS FRIED IN OIL AND GARLIC ARE SOLD ON THE STREET. LARGE SPIDERS ARE EATEN BY PEOPLE IN MANY PARTS OF THE WORLD, FROM SOUTHEAST ASIA TO SOUTH AMERICA.

On the other hand, spiders were blamed for a long-lasting epidemic of disease and madness that raged through Europe from the fourteenth to the seventeenth century. It started with a series of alleged spider bites outside the town of Taranto, in southern Italy. Supposedly, people who were bitten first felt faint, then had trouble breathing. Soon they began to tremble and shake, and before long their entire body was being wrenched into a bizarre, violent dance. Insanity, collapse, and death would follow. The only cure, people believed, was to keep the bite victims dancing until they sweated out all the spider venom. Helpful relatives and friends of the victims hired musicians to keep the dance music going and the bite victims in motion.

The suspected local spider was named the tarantula, after the town, but it was not at all related to the hairy mygalomorphs we call tarantulas today. It was actually a European wolf spider, and it was wrongly accused—this spider is incapable of causing such symptoms in humans. Historians still debate what the real cause of "tarantism" was. But the scientific name of the spider, *Lycosa tarantula*, remains to remind us of the spider's famous historical role. The epidemic did leave us one other memento: a lively folk dance, called the tarantella.

Elsewhere in the world, people have occasionally found spiders handy animals to have around. Native peoples of South America and southern Africa as well as people of Southeast Asia traditionally ate spiders. Some still do. In all regions, it appears, the largest spiders are the favorites, and barbecuing seems to be the preferred method of preparation. Many of us undoubtedly find the idea of eating a spider absolutely disgusting. But, then, most of us will eat a lobster or a crab without hesitation. What, other than custom, makes one arthropod delicious and another repulsive is unclear.

A SPIDER'S ABILITY TO TRAVEL ACROSS ANY TERRAIN AND TO SENSE THE WORLD THROUGH ITS LEGS HAS INSPIRED A VARIETY OF ROBOTS. THIS JAPANESE MODEL IS DESIGNED TO SEARCH FOR BURIED LANDMINES.

In New Guinea and several islands of the South Pacific, people used the giant webs of the silk spider to make fishing nets. They would either find a forked stick and cover it with existing webs or bend a bamboo pole into a loop and induce a silk spider to weave its web within. Then they would go fishing. Reportedly, these nets could catch fish weighing 2 to 3 pounds.

Aside from these few meetings, humans and spiders have pretty much left each other alone. Our modern attitude toward spiders is marked by fear, which is usually unjustified. Still, there *are* a few spiders of which we should be wary.

Powerful Poisoners

All spider venom is deadly—but not to humans. Spiders evolved to kill insects, not people, and their venom is generally not effective on us. All the same, a few spiders produce a poison that can affect us very badly.

In the United States the best known dangerous spider is the black widow, one of some thirty related species that live around the world. There are actually five American widow species. Three are black, one is red, one brown. But the southern black widow (*Lactrodectus mactans*), which now lives in many parts of the country besides the South, is the most widely encountered.

It is also the most powerful. The venom of a black widow spider is roughly fifteen times more potent than that of a rattlesnake. It works by causing a general, extremely painful paralysis of muscles and nervous system, and it can kill. But the real danger posed by the black widow is greatly exaggerated. Black widow spiders, like all their kin, are shy, dark-loving creatures that want nothing to do with anything as large and as inedible as a human. Experiments have shown that it takes quite a lot of prodding to get a black widow to bite something it does not regard as food. However, the spider can be provoked by being accidentally squeezed against a person's body.

Such events do happen, and fortunately there are antitoxins

A RED HOURGLASS ON ITS ABDOMEN MARKS THIS SPIDER AS A BLACK WIDOW, A
SMALL TANGLED-WEB WEAVER WITH A BIG REPUTATION AND A VENOM FIFTEEN TIMES
MORE POTENT THAN A RATTLESNAKE'S.

available to treat black widow bites. Nevertheless, the chance of being bitten by a black widow is much smaller than the chance of being hit by lightning.

The other dangerous American spider is popularly known as the brown recluse, though some people call it the violin spider—it has a violin-shaped mark on its cephalothorax. The venom of a recluse (*Loxosceles reclusa*) works differently from that of a widow. It kills tissue directly at the site of the bite rather than working on the whole nervous system. A recluse bite can be very dangerous and can result in an area of dead tissue six inches (15 cm) across.

Brown recluses can be found in many parts of the country, and there have been hundreds of reports of suspected recluse bites. In many of the reported cases, however, the person bitten actually never saw the biter; many of the other reported cases have come from areas in which no recluses live. Most likely, fear of the spider has led to this exaggeration. The real culprits may well be ticks or kissing bugs—both of which are scarier than a spider since they can transmit serious diseases. Experiments have shown that recluses too would rather not waste venom on something as big as us. They simply do not recognize us as an animal. To most spiders, a human arm might as well be a floor.

Other areas of the world also have their share of dangerous spiders, but overall they are a tiny fraction of all spider species.

Spider Potential

More important for humans than the threat posed by spiders is the possible benefit we might yet derive from these creatures. A number of researchers around the globe are studying spider venom to see if we can put it to some good use. There has long been an effort to see if spider venom can be used in insecticides that are harmless to humans and other animals. Some scientists are also looking at the possibility of making drugs from spider venom to treat conditions ranging from heart attacks to epilepsy. NASA robotics specialists are using the spider as a model for a sensor-studded walking robot that might one day make its multi-legged way over the plains of Mars.

Sadly, the chief impact we have on spiders is to deprive them of more of their natural habitat year after year. The loss of rain forests in Central and South America is the prime example, but it is not the only one. Every time that woods or fields or wetlands are developed for human use, there is a loss of natural habitat for a whole interconnected community of animals, including spiders.

Still, spiders will likely adapt. They have been here much, much longer than we have, and they will probably be here long after we are gone. The truth is, they can do perfectly well without us. All they need is a steady supply of insects, and they do not particularly care which ones.

We, on the other hand, could not do without spiders, not even for a very short while. Spiders eat an astonishing number of insects every year. By weight, they consume a total greater than the total weight of every human being on Earth. Without spiders we might soon be up to our ears in insects, quite literally. That truly is a vision worthy of the scariest Halloween.

Glossary

abdomen—the rear segment of a spider's two main body divisions

arachnid—a member of the class of arthropods that includes spiders, scorpions, daddy longlegs, mites, and ticks

araneomorph—a true spider, having fangs that move sideways; araneomorphs make up the larger of the two basic groups of spiders, mygalomorphs being the other

arthropod—a member of the largest group of animals on Earth, all of which have jointed legs and a body divided into segments; insects and spiders are the biggest arthropod groups

ballooning—flying through the air on silk threads; young spiders use ballooning to find new homes

book lung—in spiders, a breathing organ made up of a thin folded sheet of tissue that takes oxygen from the air

cephalothorax—the front part of the spider, a combined head and thorax

chelicerae—the spider's two jaws, each equipped with a fang

chitin—the hard material that forms a spider's exoskeleton

cuticle—the outer layer of the spider's skin

egg sac—a silk container in which the female spider places her eggs to hatch

hackled band—a wooly ribbon of combined sticky and nonsticky silk produced by spiders with a cribellum (a flat spinning organ)

molt—the shedding of the exoskeleton

mygalomorph—a member of the second, smaller group of spiders, which have fangs that move downward; tarantulas and trapdoor spiders are mygalomorphs

organism—an individual living thing; a single plant or animal

palp, or **pedipalp**—one of the spider's two leglike mouthparts

pedicel—the thin waist of a spider, which joins the cephalothorax and abdomen

pheromone—a chemical scent often used by male and female animals to attract each other

scopula—a pad of hairs on the feet of some spiders that gives them the ability to climb almost any smooth surface

sexual dimorphism—a significant difference in body size between males and females of the same species

species—the basic unit of classification that defines a particular type of animal or plant; to date, nearly 38,000 different spider species have been identified

spiderling—any tiny, young spider

spinneret—a hollow, fingerlike organ that a spider uses for producing silk threads; spiders usually have six spinnerets but may have seven

spinning field—the tip of a spinneret, through which the liquid silk flows

spiracle—an opening in the surface of the body of the spider that leads to one of the tracheae, the tubes that supply air

stabilimenta—broad bands of silk placed in the center of some orb webs

tarantula—any of the large, hairy mygalomorphs

thorax—in an insect, the middle of the three sections of the body, to which the legs are attached; in spiders, the thorax is combined with the head

tracheae—the air-carrying tubes in the spider's body

Species Checklist

Spiders make up a huge group of animals. There are currently nearly 38,000 spider species identified, which are gathered into more than 3,500 genera, which in turn are collected into more than 100 families.

Here is a list of some of the distinctive families:

Family	Descriptive name	Representative species

Araneomorphs

Family	Descriptive name	Representative species
Agelinidae	funnel-web spiders	*Agelenopsis pennsyvanica* (grass spider)
Araneidae	orb-web weavers	*Argiope auranti* (yellow garden spider)
Cybaeidae	water spider	*Argyroneta aquatica* (European water spider)
Deinopidae	stick spiders	*Dinopis spinosus* (ogre-faced stick spider)
Linyphiidae	sheet-web weavers	*Neriene radiata* (filmy dome spider)
Lycosidae	wolf spiders	*Lycosa punulata* (wolf spider)
Mimetidae	pirate spiders	*Mimetus Hesperus* (pirate spider)
Pholcidae	cellar spiders	*Pholcus phalangioides* (long-bodied cellar spider)
Pisauridae	fisher spiders	*Pisaurina mira* (nursery web spider)
Salticidae	jumping spiders	*Salticus scenicus* (zebra jumper spider)
Scytodidae	spitting spiders	*Scytodes thoracica* (spitting spider)

Family	Descriptive name	Representative species
Sicariidae	six-eyed sicariid spiders	*Loxosceles reclusa* (brown recluse)
Theridiidae	comb-footed spiders	*Lactrodectus mactans* (southern black widow)
Thomasidae	crab spiders	*Misumenoides formosipes* (white-banded crab spider)
Uloboridae	hackled-band orbweavers	*Uloborus glomosus* (featherlegged orb weaver)

Mygalomorphs

Family	Descriptive name	Representative species
Atypidae	purse-web spiders	*Atypus abboti* (purse-web spider)
Ctenizidae	trapdoor spiders	*Bothriocyrtum californicum* (California trapdoor spider)
Theraphosidae	tarantulas	*Brachypelma smithi* (Mexican redknee tarantula)

Further Research

Books for Young People

Conniff, Richard. *Spineless Wonders: Strange Tales from the Invertebrate World*. New York: Henry Holt and Company, Inc., 1996.

Hamilton, Virginia. *A Ring of Tricksters: Animal Tales from America, the West Indies and Africa*. New York: Blue Sky Press, 1997.

Jones, Dick. *Spider: The Story of a Predator and Its Prey*. New York: Facts on File Publications, 1986.

White, E. B. *Charlotte's Web*. New York: Harper Collins, 2003.

Videos

Webs of Intrigue, National Geographic Society, 1994.

Web Sites

Hairy pictures: Those with a strong appetite for large spiders may want to try the photo galley of the American Tarantula Society.
http://atshq.org/gallery/

Spider facts and fictions: Rod Crawford, a spider specialist at the University of Washington's Burke Museum, presents spider myths and realities.
http://www.washington.edu/burkemuseum/spidermyth/index.html

Spiders in context: The American Arachnological Society's photo gallery presents images of spiders and all their arachnid cousins. For spiders only, click on the order Araneae.
http://www.americanarachnology.org/AAS_information.html

Worldwide webs: Nick's Gallery is actually two splendid collections of photos by a spider enthusiast, one for North American spiders
http://www.loven.plus.com/nicksspiders/namain.htm
and one for European spiders
http://www.loven.plus.com/nicksspiders/gallery.htm

Bibliography

Fenton, Carroll Lane and Mildred Adams Fenton. *The Fossil Book: A Record of Prehistoric Life*. Rev. ed. New York: Doubleday, 1989.

Fortey, Richard. *Life: A Natural History of the First Four Billion Years of Life on Earth*. New York: Alfred A. Knopf, 1998.

———. *Trilobite! Eyewitness to Evolution*. New York: Alfred A. Knopf, 2000.

Gertsch, Willis J. *American Spiders*. 2nd ed. New York: Van Nostrand Reinhold Company, 1979.

Gould, Stephen Jay. *Wonderful Life: The Burgess Shale and the Nature of History*. New York: W. W. Norton & Company, 1989.

———, ed. *The Book of Life: An Illustrated History of the Evolution of Life on Earth*. New York: W. W Norton & Company, 1993.

Hillyard, Paul. *The Book of the Spider*. New York: Random House, Inc., 1994.

Preston-Mafham, Rod, and Ken Preston-Mafham. *Spiders of the World*. New York: Facts on File Publications, 1984.

Vogel, Steven. *Vital Circuits: On Pumps, Pipes, and the Workings of Circulatory Systems*. New York: Oxford University Press, 1992.

———. *Cats' Paws and Catapults: Mechanical Worlds of Nature and People*. New York: W. W. Norton & Company, 1998.

Whitfield, John. "Spider scents attract prey." Nature Science Update, http://www.nature.com/nsu/020617/020617-14.html (Accessed June 24, 2004).

Zschokke, Samuel. "Spider-web silk from the Early Cretaceous." *Nature* 424 (Accessed August 7, 2003).

Index

Page numbers in **boldface** are illustrations.

About the Author

MARC ZABLUDOFF, former editor-in-chief of *Discover* magazine, has been involved in helping to explain science to a general audience for more than twenty years. This is the first of his science books for children to be published. Others scheduled for future release by Benchmark Books include books in the AnimalWays series on beetles and monkeys, and, for the Family Trees series, titles on insects, reptiles, and the largely unknown, and chiefly microscopic, organisms known as protoctists. Zabludoff lives in New York City with his wife and daughter. Despite her initial resistance, his daughter has become an enthusiastic admirer of especially large, hairy spiders—so long as they keep their distance.